▶ National Policy in a Global Economy

DOI: 10.1057/9781137473059.0001

## Other Palgrave Pivot titles

Barend Lutz and Pierre du Toit: Defining Democracy in a Digital Age: Political Support on Social Media

Assaf Razin and Efraim Sadka: Migration States and Welfare States: Why is America Different from Europe?

Conra D. Gist: Preparing Teachers of Color to Teach: Culturally Responsive Teacher Education in Theory and Practice

David Baker: Police, Picket-Lines and Fatalities: Lessons from the Past

Lassi Heininen (editor): Security and Sovereignty in the North Atlantic

Steve Coulter: New Labour Policy, Industrial Relations and the Trade Unions

Ayman A. El-Desouky: The Intellectual and the People in Egyptian Literature and Culture: Amāra and the 2011 Revolution

William Van Lear: The Social Effects of Economic Thinking

Mark E. Schaefer and John G. Poffenbarger: The Formation of the BRICS and Its Implication for the United States: Emerging Together

Donatella Padua: John Maynard Keynes and the Economy of Trust: The Relevance of the Keynesian Social Thought in a Global Society

Davinia Thornley: Cinema, Cross-Cultural Collaboration, and Criticism: Filming on an Uneven Field

Lou Agosta: A Rumor of Empathy: Rewriting Empathy in the Context of Philosophy

Tom Watson (editor): Middle Eastern and African Perspectives on the Development of Public Relations: Other Voices

Adebusuyi Isaac Adeniran: Migration and Regional Integration in West Africa: A Borderless ECOWAS

Craig A. Cunningham: Systems Theory for Pragmatic Schooling: Toward Principles of Democratic Education

David H. Gans and Ilya Shapiro: Religious Liberties for Corporations?: Hobby Lobby, the Affordable Care Act, and the Constitution

Samuel Larner: Forensic Authorship Analysis and the World Wide Web

Karen Rich: Interviewing Rape Victims: Practice and Policy Issues in an International Context

Ulrike M. Vieten (editor): Revisiting Iris Marionyoung on Normalisation, Inclusion and Democracy

Fuchaka Waswa, Christine Ruth Saru Kilalo, and Dominic Mwambi Mwasaru: Sustainable Community Development: Dilemma of Options in Kenya

DOI: 10.1057/9781137473059.0001

palgrave▶pivot

# National Policy in a Global Economy: How Government Can Improve Living Standards and Balance the Books

Ian Budge

*Emeritus Professor of Government, Department of Government, University of Essex, UK*

with

Sarah Birch

*Chair of Comparative Politics, School of Social and Political Sciences, University of Glasgow, UK*

DOI: 10.1057/9781137473059.0001

First published 2014 by
PALGRAVE MACMILLAN

Palgrave Macmillan in the UK is an imprint of Macmillan Publishers Limited, registered in England, company number 785998, of Houndmills, Basingstoke, Hampshire RG21 6XS.

Palgrave Macmillan in the US is a division of St Martin's Press LLC, 175 Fifth Avenue, New York, NY 10010.

Palgrave Macmillan is the global academic imprint of the above companies and has companies and representatives throughout the world.

Palgrave® and Macmillan® are registered trademarks in the United States, the United Kingdom, Europe and other countries.

ISBN: 978-1-137-47306-6 EPUB
ISBN: 978-1-137-47305-9 PDF
ISBN: 978-1-137-47304-2 Hardback

A catalogue record for this book is available from the British Library.

A catalog record for this book is available from the Library of Congress.

www.palgrave.com/pivot

DOI: 10.1057/9781137473059

# Contents

palgrave▸pivot

www.palgrave.com/pivot

DOI: 10.1057/9781137473059.0001

# Introduction

Abstract: *This introduces the themes of the book, previews the main argument and provides a guide to subsequent chapters, outlining the case for a radically different approach to economic policy.*

Budge, Ian with Sarah Birch. *National Policy in a Global Economy: How Government Can Improve Living Standards and Balance the Books.* Basingstoke: Palgrave Macmillan, 2014. DOI: 10.1057/9781137473059.0002.

▶

The integration of national economies into a unified global one has vastly reduced national governments' power to shape their own economy. The diverse economic activities which take place on their territory are shaped by independent international institutions and technical developments beyond their control (the advent of digital technologies, improved mineral extraction, new antibiotics and materials, three-dimensional 'printing' of artefacts). A major problem with political parties and governments is that they continue to debate policy as though there *is* a national economy which they can 'build'. This is fundamentally a political conception, not an economic one, though it has profound implications for the way in which economic problems are understood and addressed.

This concentration on what are at best marginal interventions, and at worst ineffectual and resource-wasting policies, obscures what governments *can* do with the powers at their disposal. That is improving other areas of life within and for their own territory. Once accepted that economic growth and development are – like weather – surrounding conditions that are largely beyond the control of politicians in individual countries, a major constraint on internal policy-making is removed. With this realization government should be free to decide on policies based on their immediate contribution to the common good and not in terms of their hypothetical (but in reality unknown) consequences for medium- and long-term economic performance.

A major example is fiscal policy. It is often argued by economists and politicians that taxing multinational companies realistically will cause them to pack up and go elsewhere. Once governments accept that multinationals will make decisions on many other grounds, we can challenge this alleged constraint on their own actions. Distributor companies will not wish to lose a major market; factories cannot be abandoned without cost; good infrastructure is hard to ignore; cash-strapped governments elsewhere will follow the precedent, levelling the international playing field.

The same goes for other policy areas such as health, welfare, education, culture, sport and so on. Policies in the United Kingdom should be driven by their own merits – not because action will have hypothetical economic benefits. Making the country a better place will no doubt make it more attractive, economically, in the long term. But this should not be the policy's main justification, as business moves are so uncertain. Other European governments have already adopted such self-justifying

DOI: 10.1057/9781137473059.0002

strategies with considerable success, and Britain would be well-advised to follow their lead.

Breaking the link between national policy-making and economics should be immensely liberating for governments and beneficial for citizens. Charting fiscal policy by what you need to pay for, rather than fear of imagined consequences, provides more stability internationally and makes other benefits possible – *and* balances budgets, as is only prudent in the face of unpredictable global change.

This is the gist of the book's argument. It aims to develop a radical alternative to the conventional thinking of all the main parties, also propagated by many political and economic commentators. This alternative is underpinned by our analysis of current trends. But the argument cannot be altogether constrained by these trends as its purpose is to suggest other ways of tackling them. Thus when we suggest a social partnership rather than the non-negotiable stance taken by most governments at the present time, we are pointing to alternatives freed from Keynesian or even neo-liberal economics based on the myth of a controllable national economy. Britain will be used as the prime example in the book, though the analysis applies in a wide variety of contexts (except possibly the United States – the one reasonably autonomous national economy in the world).

The separate chapters develop these points in more detail, starting in Chapter 1 with our current situation and the way it has been interpreted by economists and politicians, media commentators and reporters. The chapter expands on our analysis, arguing that the 'national economy' has little meaning other than as the government's (potential) tax base. Peculiarly, economic analysis and discussion has adopted a political rather than an economic definition of an 'economy', and we ought to recognize this and follow through on its implications.

In Chapter 2 we review the scholarly literature on the phenomenon labelled 'globalization', which has ended national economic autonomy. We assess evidence on its nature and effects, before looking at the implications of a globalized economy for recent economic developments in Britain.

This brings us on to Chapter 3, 'What National Governments Can and Can't Do Well', which reinforces the point that government has little influence over the level of economic activity on its territory, given globalization. It is still the major economic actor there but not a dynamic one. What it *can* do is see to the well-being of its population

DOI: 10.1057/9781137473059.0002

under unpredictable and uncontrollable conditions, as with the weather.

This is the theme of Chapter 4, 'Providing Citizen Support'. To maximize well-being, governments need to get their priorities sorted out. There should be essential provision for security, health, welfare, education, culture and the environment. Aiming at high levels of provision in these areas may have long-term economic benefits. But these benefits are not assured, and action should be aimed at short- and medium-term payoffs for citizens. An essential is a universal guarantee of adequate income.

The weakness of most schemes for state support is specifying how they can be paid for. We deal with this in Chapter 5, which suggests two concrete ways of balancing the books:

1  Revising expenditure priorities, shedding non-essentials such as a world military and diplomatic presence; a large prison population; transport and tax subsidies (including bank bailouts)
2  Taxing all economic activity in the country equally, taking in multinationals

The chapter argues that this is feasible since governments still have the political power to do such things in their own territory. This is unlikely to produce a flight of capital since:

▸ other national governments will follow suit; and
▸ multinationals find it hard to move.

Exit from the EU forms a current example of a decision being considered by politicians without much regard to economic consequences – even if it is probably more important to multinationals to be in the common market than to be taxed (effectively) on the same footing as purely national companies.

All of this adds up to a non-partisan programme putting ordinary people at the heart of things (Chapter 6). This presents our proposals directly and simply in the shape of an election manifesto of the kind most readers will be familiar with. Its proposals are hardly original, as popular protest movements throughout Europe threw up these ideas in a variety of books and pamphlets in 2012–13. Establishment figures often dismissed these as a rag-bag of unconnected demands. Chapter 7 takes them seriously and finds them linked by a convincing underlying rationale (related of course to our arguments made earlier). With governments

DOI: 10.1057/9781137473059.0002

trumpeting economic success as they take credit for a slight global upturn in business activity, it is ever more apparent that waiting for events and taking credit for them (or avoiding blame) is just a device for avoiding responsibility for what they *can* do. The chapter drives home this point by recapitulating our previous argument, which adds up to asserting the primacy of politics – particularly parties – and the need for them to stop claiming credit for global economic developments while taking over responsibility for improving life where they can act freely – within their own country.

There is a bit of a paradox in arguing that national governments' inability to do much about the economy actually frees them to act more decisively in other areas. There is no real inconsistency, however, since economic panaceas have so often been used as reasons for inaction or even withdrawal from crucial areas of national life. Chapter 1 now goes into these points in more detail, providing a reasoned basis for the recommendations we make further on in the book.

DOI: 10.1057/9781137473059.0002

# 1
# A British Economy?
# Boxing with Shadows

**Abstract:** *This chapter argues that the notion of a 'British economy' is a myth in today's globalized world. This has considerable implications for governments' approaches to dealing with economic crisis. The underlying problems with the classic 'austerity' and Keynesian approaches will be elaborated. The focus will be mainly on Britain, though there will also be references to austerity measures implemented elsewhere.*

Keywords: austerity politics; British economy; economic crisis; globalization; Keynesianism

Budge, Ian with Sarah Birch. *National Policy in a Global Economy: How Government Can Improve Living Standards and Balance the Books.* Basingstoke: Palgrave Macmillan, 2014. DOI: 10.1057/9781137473059.0003.

In the *Non-Existent Knight*, a moral tale by Italo Calvino, the Emperor Charlemagne is reviewing his knights, flicking up their visors to see what condition they are in after an exhausting campaign. One suit of armour has nobody inside. 'Good God man, how do you keep going?' cries the Emperor. 'Persistence and faith in our holy cause.'

The same could be said of the British economy. It doesn't really exist but economists persist in talking as if it does, and politicians share their faith in it. There are endless plans for its revitalization. In party pledges and programmes it takes the central part, with promises to generate more wealth from a recovery that will create jobs for everyone and pay for everything else – if only we will put up with cuts and austerity (or, alternatively, inflation) for some time yet. As another poet remarked, 'I see the bridle and the spurs of course – but where's the bloody horse?'

None of this is to deny that there are economic activities going on in Britain which provide most of the population with a living and generate the revenues which pay for government and for public goods and services. Of course there are. We would be flying in the face of reality to deny it. But do such activities cohere with each other and add up to an economy in the sense of a set of activities and enterprises which have more to do with each other than they do with ones located outside their boundaries? If they do not – as we will argue is clearly the case in Britain and most contemporary states – how can the British government claim to steer them and plan for their future as a coherent autonomous entity rather than a more or less random agglomeration which does not respond consistently to government signals? If the oil industry has more links with Norway or Arabia than with Midlands car manufacturing; if London banks make more money from speculating in America than in Europe – let alone Britain; if agriculture is shaped more by the Common Agricultural Policy of the European Union (EU) than by British regulation, where are the communalities that bind all these activities (and many more) together, other than the fact that they all happen to be located in Britain (but spread also over a lot of other places)? This lack of economic cohesion is not of course peculiar to Britain. It is true of most countries in the world. Only in a few large ones – the United States and perhaps India – could the economic enterprises located there be said to have more to do with each other than with the rest of the world. Even mighty exporters like China and Japan have by that very fact made themselves dependent on distribution chains and sales elsewhere and so rely on other countries' efficiency and prosperity for their own economic health.

DOI: 10.1057/9781137473059.0003

The major factor unifying so-called national economies is para-doxically a political one: they share the same overall government. This is usually the largest single economic actor within its own territory, and it makes some rules for the others. But even that role is being eroded by international agreements and treaties.

The most realistic definition of a so-called national economy is that it is the national governments' potential tax base, from which it can draw the revenues to finance its other activities – wars and administration but also some public services (all themselves, of course, 'economic activities' of some kind). All this might seem academic. What does it matter to ordinary folk how you define an economy? What does matter is that there are decent jobs and wages and reasonable living conditions. So long as the enterprises and firms in a country provide these, who cares whether they have more to do with each other than with other parts of a corporation located abroad?

We shall argue that it does matter – that it makes a big difference to our personal well-being if national policy-makers think they can make economic plans untrammelled by external developments and events and demand national sacrifices for doing so. The idea of an autonomous national economy which they can shape at will clearly encourages reck-less government behaviour. Dashes for growth and grandiose plans for expansion are too often succeeded by austerity and service cuts to 'rebalance the books' – itself a somewhat dubious concept highly shaped by arbitrary and obscure accounting conventions (Sikka, 2010). Our sad experience of so many development plans which came unstuck has alas made few dents in governments' endless optimism. In this they are encouraged by their economic gurus, neo-liberal or Keynesian, who generally claim to have an economic panacea which will – eventually – work within the national context.

Unfortunately these ambitious economic plans usually come at the cost of neglecting the other things governments could do to improve life nationally. In particular, health, education, culture, sports and environ-ment often take a beating as they are viewed in purely economic terms or as unnecessary fripperies in the context of the latest wheeze for national economic growth. 'Paradise postponed' should be the notice on most chancellors' doors.

We should move away from government-led economic development. In a country like Britain economic development has already arrived and will take care of itself. In any case governments have demonstrated

DOI: 10.1057/9781137473059.0003

quite clearly that they cannot deliver it – though they rarely fail to claim the credit for any surge in activity due, for example, to the discovery of oil, or the irresponsible actions of banks, while blaming others for downturns.

What national governments should be doing instead is what does lie within their power to improve things – charge efficiently for their business services and then spend adequately on the general quality of life for their citizens. They *do* have control over their own territory. But they often neglect service improvements in the here and now to pursue some economic vision for the distant future.

In the following chapters we will provide arguments and evidence to support our thesis, ending with a practical plan of action which focuses much of the political debate which has taken place since the world economic collapse of 2008. We start by expanding on what we have said here, beginning with a diagnosis of the thinking of professional economists which has encouraged national governments to go up the blind alley of seeking to promote economic growth.

# Defining economies politically: a basic flaw in macroeconomic analysis

How would we react if lawyers insisted on studying 'Iberian' law, ignoring the division of the peninsula into Spain and Portugal, with separate Parliaments, law codes and courts? Or if they claimed that Russian law operated differently in the European area and in Siberia, ignoring the fact that the Russian Federation covers both? We would clearly feel there was something wrong if lawyers took natural geographic features as defining their basic unit of analysis, rather than as an area under one sovereign legislative authority.

Why therefore should we accept economists taking politically defined entities – states – as their basic unit rather than one which makes sense in economic terms? As we have suggested, taking an economically rather than a politically defined unit for analysis would lead to a macro-economic focus on clusters of economic activities which actually belonged together, in the sense that their interactions were more focused on each other than on outside activity. Economies defined in this way would indeed be largely autonomous entities whose dynamics – their growth and contraction – would be driven largely by internal developments

DOI: 10.1057/9781137473059.0003

rather than by events elsewhere. Such internal developments might of course include government interventions and fiscal policy, which could have a considerable effect if the economy were largely self-contained.

Few economies of course are like Robinson Crusoe on his island, totally self-contained. However clusters with more transactions taking place internally would approximate this favoured example. The 'national' economies usually referred to actually lack any clear economic boundary, so that in practice their economic activity is just a local manifestation of a larger economy whose dynamics are determined by wider forces than those operating locally.

Most, if not all, national economies are now edging closer to the latter than to the former situation, that is, their expansions and contractions are driven to a great extent by external forces. True, so-called gravity and border effects do mean that most trade takes place within states or with close neighbours (Anderson and Wincoop, 2004; Helliwell, 1998). Yet there is evidence that this effect has declined over time (Parsley and Wei, 2001). Certainly most goods and services bought and sold by UK economic actors involve domestic trade only – two-thirds in fact. However this also implies that one-third does not. In 2012, 34 per cent of all goods and services consumed within the United Kingdom came from abroad, and 32 per cent of all the goods and services produced in the United Kingdom were exported.[1] These are the more dynamic flows more directly affecting internal economic developments, for example, supermarkets searching for ever cheaper food from abroad. Only in the movement of labour do cross-border restrictions and cultural impediments significantly limit cross-border flows. Even these factors have diminished considerably in recent years within the European Union.

The 'new institutionalist' political economy, which became popular in the 1990s, does put emphasis on the role of domestic institutions in structuring economic activity (e.g., Coase, 1998; North, 1990; Ostrom, 2005). However evidence suggests that the relevance of national institutions is overplayed. Figure 1.1 demonstrates the extent to which economic growth in the United Kingdom tracks developments elsewhere in the world, and particularly among comparators such as the OECD and EU member states.

It is telling that growth rates in other parts of the world are better predictors of what happens in the UK economy than are official predictions made by UK state agencies whose task it is to forecast economic developments. Figure 1.2 demonstrates the frequent discrepancy between

DOI: 10.1057/9781137473059.0003

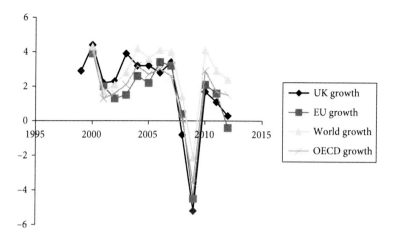

**FIGURE 1.1**     *UK growth is global growth*

*Note*: The data in this table are based on the 'GDP growth (annual %)' indicator from the World Bank's World Development Indicators dataset at www.worldbank.org. This measure reflects the 'annual percentage growth rate of GDP at market prices based on constant local currency. Aggregates are based on constant 2005 U.S. dollars'.

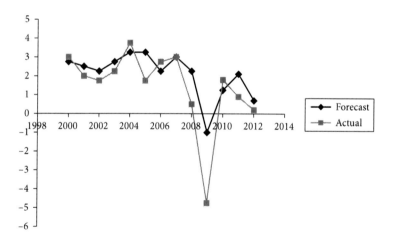

**FIGURE 1.2**     *Forecast and actual growth in the United Kingdom, 2000–12*

*Note*: These data were obtained from the following sources: forecasts are those made by the Treasury and reported in pre-Budget Reports/Autumn Statements (http://webarchive. nationalarchives.gov.uk/20100407010852/http://www.hm-treasury.gov.uk/prebud_pbr05_ index.htm); actual growth rates are those reported by the Treasury and the Office for Budget Responsibility (http://budgetresponsibility.org.uk/category/topics/economic-forecasts/).

DOI: 10.1057/9781137473059.0003

economic forecasts and resulting change over recent years. The forecast is almost always higher than the reality, possibly owing to political pressures.

It is clear from these figures that the efforts of domestic policy-makers to steer economic development in the United Kingdom are often unsuccessful. Actual growth rates are determined largely by what happens outside the borders of the United Kingdom. The pattern of correlation coefficients between these sets of figures backs up this claim. There is a coefficient of .93 between UK and EU growth rates over this period and a coefficient of .94 between UK growth and OECD growth.[2] The correlation between UK growth and world growth is .89. The correlation coefficient between Treasury predictions for the next year and actual growth for that year is, at .86, lower than all of these. In other words we would do better basing ourselves on world growth to anticipate what is going to happen in the United Kingdom than on government actions and aspirations. This provides strong evidence that the efforts of UK leaders to steer British economic activity have less influence on economic outcomes than do global economic forces, and especially economic forces from the United Kingdom's closest trading partners.

This new reality has two implications: (a) simulations and predictions of the way the country will develop economically have to have accurate information about the impact that wider forces have on internal activities – not just on those in closely linked sectors but in each of the diverse sectors represented in a given territory. We do not simply need to know about how Chinese imports will impact generally on Britain but what impact they will have, for example, on pharmaceuticals or sales of toys, heavy machinery or furniture-making. The cruder and less sensitive this type of information is, the less accurate will be our predictions of what is going to happen in the relevant area. Quite apart from prediction, we may not even be able to see what is happening now, in the necessary detail. (b) This in turn means that governments have too little information about what is actually happening on the ground, economically speaking, in their own territory. They have little basis for informed action, therefore, other than crude general ideas, for example, that pumping out more money will encourage sales. As seen so often in Britain, however, these will often be sales of foreign imports and so do little to stimulate home employment, outside the distributor companies. So the intended effects – stimulating growth and jobs – tend to materialize only in a muted way, if at all. Medium-term effects can be

DOI: 10.1057/9781137473059.0003

perverse, resulting in an overall loss of jobs in small firms making these products in Britain.

The wider problem, however, is that by talking in terms of a national economy (by implication one with a largely internal, autonomous dynamic) many economists encourage governments to think they can produce intended and significant effects. The reality is of course that they rarely can do so. They may be the big fish in the national pond – though even there they are not typically the most dynamic or adept economic actors. But they are small fish indeed in Europe or in the world.

Why do most economists not base themselves on a more realistic unit of analysis to which their theories would apply – that is, an economy driven by its own internal dynamics in a relatively predictable way rather than one shaken by the external forces which predominate in its workings? In the presence of globalization this might imply working at the world level, given that every area is now so interdependent with others. But if this is the only way to generate a realistic macro-model, whose predictions can then be applied to different countries depending on the particular mix of economic activities going on there – why not?

The answer may lie in a certain professional inertia. National governments are the major bodies collecting statistics on economic activities, with international bodies like the OECD (Organization for Economic Co-operation and Development) drawing on them. OECD countries have certain common standards but many outside countries do not. Non-comparable standards in classifying trade-flows and revenues contribute to notorious problems, like the 'black hole' between world imports and exports. Figures for those should logically equal each other. But often they do not, leading one to doubt the accuracy of the whole set of statistics on which they are based (*Economist*, 2013a).

National statistics, particularly for developed countries, are thus the most accurate and convenient to use. So they *are* used. But they relate to a territorially defined, politically delineated entity not to one which necessarily makes sense in terms of economics. What can be measured is studied (and therefore is assumed to exist). What cannot be measured is not studied and by extension does not exist – at any rate in the minds of most economists and politicians.

What emerges from this situation is a vicious circle. Governments keep records, for the most part, for administrative purposes. Imports, exports, incomes, profits are all crucial information about their tax base and what they can expect in the way of the revenues which they can extract as taxes from economic activities on their own territory. Yet these then provide data – often the only data – for analysis of an 'economy'. Economists therefore analyse them. Essentially the figures describe the government's potential tax base. The economic interest which drives the analysis transcends the purely administrative concern, however, and extends to fleshing out theories of how economies work. Thus the analyses have to be justified as relating to a 'national economy' even though this is defined politically. Ironically politicians then pick up the idea that there *is* in some sense a 'national economy' which they can shape. This then sets the stage for the kind of interventions and mis-management identified earlier, often destabilizing in themselves and diverting attention from the more modest but much more valuable activity governments could undertake in areas such as health education and welfare, which we describe in Chapter 3.

# How did we get here?

We will back up these points in greater detail with an analysis of globalization and the emergence of a global economy in Chapter 2. It is interesting here to see exactly how and why the British economy merged into the world one. Analyzing this process shows that it is irreversible as it is based on structural and institutional features at the heart of British society and politics.

Victorian and Imperial Britain – the first industrial nation – was in fact the carrier of globalization to the rest of the world – the centre of the world financial and trading system from the mid-nineteenth to the early twentieth century. This process was driven by its own internal economic development, leading to the abolition of protective tariffs on food imports (the Repeal of the Corn Laws in 1846). This represented a victory of the professional and new industrial bourgeoisie over the old land-owning classes which paved the way for rapid industrial and colonial expansion.

The new middle classes followed this by abolishing all protective taxes on imports. The reason they wanted to open up the economy in this way was simple. British industry was incomparably bigger and more efficient than those in other countries and therefore had nothing to fear from competition or imports. What manufacturers did want, however, was cheap food for their workforce, so that wages and prices could be kept

DOI: 10.1057/9781137473059.0003

down. Protective tariffs on food imports left prices high, to the benefit of British farmers and country dwellers in general. The abolition of tariffs on wheat signalled the end of all such protective measures, marking the dominance of urban interests over rural and of the new middle class (the 'bourgeoisie') over the landed gentry.

The abolition of protective tariffs produced the 'Great Transformation' of British society and of Britain's place in the world. For the first time a country took the gamble of making itself dependent on foreign imports for its basic survival. By the beginning of the twentieth century half of what the British ate was imported, much of it from the Americas and Australasia. This meant in turn that Britain had to export to survive. (It also rendered it particularly vulnerable in the First and Second World Wars to submarine attacks, which sank the ships that carried food into the country.)

This military consequence was not foreseen by the theorists and political agitators who attacked protection. They were, however, quite prepared to gamble on manufactured exports paying for food imports. Given British industrial supremacy, this seemed a safe bet. In support of Corn Law Repeal they developed a series of interlocking arguments for free trade, that is, the abolition of all protective tariffs on a worldwide basis.

The free trade advocates believed that without 'artificial' tariffs, the pressure of competition would force each area of the world to concentrate on what it produced most efficiently. Efficiency might be linked to natural advantages such as the presence of minerals or a beneficent climate. It was marked in practice by the ability to produce and market the good at a lower price than elsewhere in the world, provided political barriers like tariffs did not distort market judgements. Hence the importance of eliminating them.

In this way universal free markets would stimulate the production of goods and distribute them at the lowest possible prices, thereby maximizing human well-being. They also reduced the possibility of war, whose prime cause was thought to be poverty or covetousness. Now the populations of all countries would enjoy all the benefits which were humanly attainable so they would have no good reason for attacking others – or so the argument went.

The free traders argued that Britain was uniquely placed to ensure the spread of open markets in three ways. Firstly, it could set a potent example as the dominant trading nation. Secondly, it could establish free trade throughout its extensive colonial empire and force other, less developed countries, like China and the Latin American states, to open up their markets. Thirdly, its unchallengeable navy could police markets and trade routes to ensure that free trade was not threatened.

Free trade, free markets and free competition constitute a set of ideas to which British politicians and parties have been strongly attached ever since the mid-nineteenth century. Concrete examples of their continuing influence today are British membership of the European Union (conceived as an extended 'Common Market'), and enthusiasm for opening up world trade in the General Agreement on Taxes and Tariffs (GATT) and subsequently the World Trade Organization (WTO). World trading conditions and British economic competitiveness have changed enormously since the mid-nineteenth century. Regardless of such changes, British policy-makers have opened up the country to foreign trade and done their best to abolish protection internationally, apart from a brief period during the economic recession of the 1930s.

The explanation for this steadfast adherence to free trade and economic liberalism is not simply historical and cultural but also institutional and structural. In the period of its industrial and commercial supremacy, Britain created institutions such as the financial markets in the 'City' and made enormous overseas investments which depended on world free trade and the unhampered flow of money.

These developments followed naturally from Britain's overwhelming dominance of the nineteenth-century world economy. With industrial products which nobody else was producing, and which could not all be absorbed by the domestic market, manufacturers depended on overseas outlets. But clearly something needed to be traded for manufactured goods. Other countries could go into debt, of course, and many did, contributing to a massive growth of British assets overseas. Ultimately however they needed to balance their imports with exports.

The abolition of protection in Britain, under the influence of free trade ideas, helped solve the problem. Increasingly, Britain imported food and raw materials for industry (such as raw cotton, timber and mineral ores). The most plentiful supplies of these were in the less developed world, notably North and especially South American, and Australasia. As a result, British trade turned increasingly towards these areas. In line with free trade ideas about each country doing what it did best, Britain manufactured, while overseas trading partners raised animals and crops,

DOI: 10.1057/9781137473059.0003

or dug and quarried, exploiting the extensive natural resources which they had and Britain did not.

There was a snag, however. Often the natural resources were inaccessible or under the control of hostile governments or indigenous peoples who had no desire to trade. To deal with the latter Britain rapidly expanded its direct control of likely territories, converting them into 'colonies'. It used its Navy to protect trade routes and the Army to destroy indigenous opposition.

In other cases it supported like-minded governments who could subdue the indigenous inhabitants. In terms of transport, British banks could supply capital for building railways for the transport of settlers and crops. These were usually built by British-owned companies, which used British iron for the rails, imported locomotives and rolling stock from Britain and employed British personnel, thus creating another British asset overseas.

British banks and financial institutions thus traded and invested on a world scale long before any other country did. They were driven on by the logic of an expanding economy which demanded outlets overseas and gave them immense resources for investment. The profits generated internally by British industry were such that industrial expansion up to the late nineteenth century was self-financed from profits rather than by direct borrowing from banks. Hence, to use their deposits profitably, financial institutions increasingly found it expedient to invest overseas.

Free trade ideas fitted these arrangements very well, justifying the world movement of capital and payment of interest back to Britain. They underpinned a situation in which investment in British industry was simply one of a number of alternative options for banks and finance houses, to be weighed against US railways, Chinese textile factories or Argentinean cattle ranches. The City naturally chose the one whose return was higher, claiming that it would be failing in its duty to maximize returns to shareholders if it did otherwise. These attitudes are still prevalent today.

Britain was able to accept universal free trade in the nineteenth century because its industry and commerce could take on the world. This was an attitude typical of the first industrialized county but which was obviously much harder for later-developing ones to accept. Primary overseas producers of food and raw materials could accept it for a while. They had products to export which Britain wanted, and by accepting the role of Britain's suppliers they could attract investment and build up

DOI: 10.1057/9781137473059.0003

their economic infrastructure of roads, railways, houses and supporting facilities.

However, other European countries had interests which directly conflicted with those of Britain. Military monarchies, like Germany and Austria, wanted to build up an industrial base in order to service their armies. It was intolerable to them that the steel they needed to make guns should not be under their control; nor that the railways needed for rapid mobilization should be maintained and run by foreign contractors. Quite apart from their military concerns, these countries also wanted to develop an industrial base for tax and revenue. By becoming richer they were able to afford bigger and better-equipped armies, which they could then use to build up their power or to defend themselves from their neighbours.

Most European countries, therefore, had strong incentives to develop their own industry. In order to do this they had to subsidize and protect them from British competition, which would (initially at any rate) have driven their products from the market. These governments, therefore, embarked on a series of measures collectively known as 'protectionism', which went directly counter to all the doctrines of free trade. Banks were directed to support national industries and close links were created between them and firms, to the extent that they even nominated their own senior staff to the firms' boards of directors. Taxes were imposed on imports, above all on British goods, to ensure that their price was higher than that of the national product. Instead of allowing market demand to determine which products would be supplied, governments indicated which industrial sectors were to be developed.

Germany was the major exponent of protectionism in the late nineteenth century, but all the developed countries apart from Britain followed suit. The United States adopted a halfway policy. It protected products like steel, where it wanted to build up its own industry, but it welcomed British investment in railways and transport and was happy to supply primary products, like raw cotton or tobacco from the South, where there was a British demand.

In contrast to Germany, British industry increasingly looked for its finance not to local banks but to the Stock Exchange, where company shares were bought and sold. By extending the idea of a limited liability company – where the maximum individual investors could lose was the value of their holding in the company – the modernized exchanges increased the incentives for individuals with money to buy and sell

DOI: 10.1057/9781137473059.0003

company shares as their price fluctuated. Such individuals were not actively concerned with the development of the company they bought into. They were simply concerned with the price they could sell the shares for. If it fell, they sold rapidly, causing a general collapse of the price.

This development could bankrupt a company by preventing it from raising money through share sales or bank loans (since banks would not lend to a company in trouble). Share prices might fall for many reasons other than bad management, for example, a temporary fall in demand which, given time, a firm might overcome. Or companies might wish to invest more of their profits in better machinery to increase profits in later years.

The divorce in Britain between investment and management meant that the predominant concern of investors was the current share price, not the underlying performance and prospects of the company. If it failed to pay out high returns each year, it would be in trouble, regardless of whether it could envisage an upturn in the future. Such 'short-termism' on the part of investors has often been criticized and seen as a weakness (e.g., Hutton, 1995). As a result, manufacturing firms are always tied to immediate results and hampered from making long-term plans for modernization, research and investment to deal effectively with competition. One can see, however, that British investors are simply following the logic of a free market. Investors themselves would be in trouble if they let considerations other than immediate profit and loss enter into their consideration.

This was particularly true for British financial markets as the world was opened up from 1850 onwards, largely through their investments. Banks, insurance companies and individual investors had an increasing choice between various overseas outlets, with high and immediate rates of return. These were guaranteed by British naval and military power in the world free-trade system centred in London.

British industrial shares came late into the financial markets in any large quantity. This was because it was easier financing expansion from their high rate of profits rather than from loans or share sales. The development of more and more sophisticated – and expensive – technology increasingly ruled this option out. Profits themselves were cut into by a slow-down in the rate of growth during the 'Great Depression' of 1870–92. Firms amalgamated in order to survive. The new conglomerates turned to banks and the Stock Exchange to finance development by selling their shares.

DOI: 10.1057/9781137473059.0003

In doing so, however, they made themselves subject to the short-term pressures of the financial markets. It is in this development that we can trace the structural impact of Britain's primacy in the Industrial Revolution on the present-day situation. Had Britain not been the first to industrialize, had its investors not developed a free international financial market on the basis of British dominance, banks and finance might have co-operated with home industry rather than simply trading in it, against other options. Once such relationships took root, however, attempts to overturn them were likely to provoke a financial crisis.

Britain inherited, from the nineteenth century, financial markets that are highly efficient, internationally oriented and divorced from British industry. A better appreciation of the consequences can be obtained by comparing them in more detail with the very different path other countries, particularly Germany and Japan, took towards industrialization.

The second, third and fourth industrializing nations could not follow the free trade path marked out by Britain. To open their markets to free competition simply meant that cheaper British products would ruin their home industry. If they wanted to build their own industrial base they had to protect developing industries by imposing taxes on any incoming products that threatened them. This meant that the home consumer had to pay higher prices. On the other hand, the industries protected in this way also provided growing opportunities for employment and domestic prosperity.

The move to protection in these countries also gained strength from their desire to safeguard agriculture and home supplies of food. This was because countries like France and Germany viewed the economy above all from a military point of view. They wanted industrialization to provide steel and guns, uniforms and equipment for the army. They wanted railways to speed general mobilization and to take troops more quickly where they were needed. A productive home agricultural base was necessary for two reasons: to maintain a large, peasant population which could provide army conscripts and to ensure food supplies in time of war.

The economic policies adopted by the Continental countries were thus in complete antithesis to Britain's internationally focused free trade, where home industry had to compete with foreign imports and investment opportunities. The concern was rather to protect and nurture home industry and agriculture and to allow international competition only when these were strong enough to sustain themselves.

DOI: 10.1057/9781137473059.0003

This contrast in attitudes affects present-day relationships, particularly between Britain and its partners in the European Union. For Britain, the attraction of the Union has always been the prospect of abolishing tariffs and extending free markets across Europe, as a preliminary to extending them to the rest of the world. France and Germany, on the other hand, have always seen the Union primarily in terms of building a strong Europe which can protect and develop its industries on a Continental rather than a national scale. The British preference for a looser economic association rather than a federal union stems from the structure and functioning of its financial markets inherited from the nineteenth century.

Building up industry inside one's own country rather than through international competition also involved a different relationship with banks and financial institutions. The latter did not have the overseas investment opportunities open to the City of London, which had already monopolized them. Developing domestic industry thus offered the best way for French and German banks to make money. However, this had to be a long-term process, since the firms needed to build themselves up. In return for investments and loans firms could not offer quick profits. Instead they provided seats on their boards for bank representatives and other shareholders and involved them in the day-to-day management of the business.

Instead of 'short-termism', therefore, second-stage industrialization encouraged 'long-termism'. Shares were not bought and traded as commodities but conserved as part of a permanent relationship between shareholders and managers, and profits were to be taken only after the business could afford it. Investment and modernization were seen as a continuing process necessary for future development and continuing viability.

Long-term planning was encouraged through the active intervention of the government in these relationships. Economic strength was seen as a national priority, even as a prerequisite for national survival. This encouraged a much more active role for government – also in the social sphere – than in Britain, where free trade doctrines limited government intervention as much as possible, in order to allow markets to operate at maximum efficiency.

It is important to see these contrasts between Britain and other countries not just as accidental, but as rooted in the structures and institutions that followed from the sequence of industrialization in the world.

DOI: 10.1057/9781137473059.0003

Being first, British practices and attitudes necessarily differed from most of those countries which developed later. What has shaped society, economics, and politics cannot be reversed without fundamental revolution, which Britain has never had and is unlikely to have.

Like all complex historical developments, this one had both positive and negative effects. British attachment to free trade has rendered the financial sector notably competitive at a world level. The City of London is one of four leading financial markets in the world (along with New York, Frankfurt and Tokyo). On the negative side, British industry has been unprotected and undercapitalized. As manufacturing industry generally employs more people than finance, this meant that the bulk of the population, particularly in regions outside the Southeast of England, suffered greatly from closures and unemployment, leading to insecurity and poverty in their lives.

By 1900 British economic activities were firmly linked with global ones which they no longer effortlessly dominated. The 'Great Depression' itself, extending over the last three decades of the nineteenth century, was a symptom of the adjustments taking place. Due to improved transport and communication the main British banks and enterprises no longer dealt primarily with each other but with foreign counterparts scattered round the globe. What ended the Depression were two *international* developments. Firstly, there was an upturn in world demand for all sorts of goods and services, owing to increasing wealth and activity as economies developed. Secondly, there was an increase in international tensions as Germany took Britain's dominant position in a variety of areas. These resulted in an armaments race which temporarily at least revived British heavy industry and increasingly integrated sectors with each other, duplicating for the moment the domestic investment and integration which full scale protectionism had created elsewhere.

However, the disruption to world trade created by the First World War and abrupt cessation of military spending after its conclusion created another acute Depression in Britain. British economic activity was by now so firmly tied into world activity that the protectionist measures belatedly adopted by successive governments were largely ineffective. Only renewed re-armament at home and abroad and then war itself created a renewed demand for goods and services. The world stimulus continued till about 1970 since the Second World War destroyed so much in the way of equipment and infrastructure that even inefficient British firms and manufacturers found markets for their products.

DOI: 10.1057/9781137473059.0003

Yet parallel to their ineffective economic interventions British governments did provide protections for their citizens against the unpredictable upturns and down-swings of the world economy – free education, welfare and health. These were to prove more enduring and effective than attempts at economic amalgamation and planning, which largely broke down in the world oil crisis of the 1970s, or nationalization of energy and communications, which were sold off in the 1980s. Private ownership and Free Trade again became the economic panacea from the mid-1980s, until they helped produce the financial crash of 2008 and world economic recession thereafter, from which we are only slowly emerging.

The traditionally protectionist countries – France, Italy, Germany and Spain – fared somewhat better than Britain as they recovered from the immediate aftermath of war. Their enforced investment in up-to-date machinery and plants boosted exports, while protectionist practices safeguarded domestic enterprises. Germany, indeed, thrived so much under these conditions that it was able to absorb and modernize the former East Germany – a quarter of the newly reconstituted country – without excessive strain in the 1990s. Indeed the German-dominated zone stretching from the Low Countries into Central Europe has claims to be one of the few surviving autonomous economies in the world today. This accounts for Germany's greater ability to weather world recessions and maintain a relatively stable economy and society in spite of the upheavals of the last quarter of a century.

For the Mediterranean countries the opposite is true, as free trade increasingly brings foreign goods and services into the heart of domestic life and their internal activities fail or get absorbed by multinational corporations. In a sense, therefore, British practices of Free Trade and the dominance of a world-wide financial sector have won out. Even the European Union, which started out as a protectionist bloc of countries that opened themselves up to each other but kept outsiders away, has become a free trade advocate, negotiating tariff reductions with North America and China, which if successful will integrate most of its members into world trading networks and make them dependent on world finance.

Meanwhile the United States has replaced Britain at the core of the world economy. In doing so it has gone down the same path as Britain had previously followed. Finance and the share-markets have increasingly divorced themselves from domestic industry, as American

DOI: 10.1057/9781137473059.0003

companies become multinational ones operating simultaneously at many levels across a range of countries. For the moment the system largely operates to America's advantage as the dollar forms the medium of exchange and transactions largely take place on American terms. However, dependency cuts both ways. The United States can only decreasingly isolate itself from world recession, while China, India and other recently industrialized countries take over many areas of manufacturing.

## How should national government react?

British powerlessness to influence world economic developments playing out on its territory means that the traditional policies both of the Left and the Right have become outmoded. For example, the idea that cheap food and low wages will somehow increase the competitiveness of the few remaining British firms has been overtaken by the fact that such measures disproportionately benefit multinationals operating on British soil which bring in overseas goods to sell in Britain. Purely British firms are more likely to be niche survivors drawing on the traditional strengths of well-paid and qualified workers to produce quality goods for which they have a small but steady market.

On the other hand this gives little scope for the Keynesian policies traditionally favoured by the Left. J.M. Keynes (1883–1946) believed that governments could revive a flagging domestic economy by increasing the money supply, for example, by spending savings, running a deficit or printing new money ('quantitative easing'). Increased government spending on capital projects would then give firms more opportunities and work. This in turn would lead to 'overheating'. When this happened, national governments could go into reverse, call in debt and reduce the money supply, calming down growth and development and thereby avoiding a hectic boom followed by a cataclysmic bust, which would produce another recession.

Governments – anxious to spend and gain popularity – have, however, proved notably bad at regulating spending, which they have always done far too late. This produced the stop-go policies of the 1950s and the 1960s as governments belatedly took their foot off the economic accelerator and then drastically cut spending, bankrupting over-extended firms and individuals.

DOI: 10.1057/9781137473059.0003

By the 1970s however government ineptness in applying such controls was no longer the main problem. Keynesian policies themselves ceased to work. Hyper-inflation coexisted with unprecedented post-war unemployment, which remained high however fast inflation increased.

Keynesianism is an appealing theory which was long the prevailing orthodoxy. Its failure, in particular within the British context, is not due so much to flaws in the general theory as to the fact that the theory is not being applied to a self-contained economy. It is no longer a question of balancing domestic supply and demand. One needs to balance world supply and demand as they affect Britain. And that is clearly a task beyond any national government (Scharpf, 2013).

No solution however was to be found in old ideas of financial austerity, cutting public expenditure and restricting the money supply to restore stability and confidence. Only the unanticipated discovery and extraction of North Sea oil by international companies provided a necessary boost which, in conjunction with a world recovery, slowly increased activity and reduced unemployment by the end of the 1980s. The same might be said of the current recession (2008–14). Domestic policies of monetary expansion and austerity failed to counter depressed activity in Britain until Europe and the world themselves began to recover.

The current solution favoured by the Right (but reluctantly accepted also on the Left) is to make Britain more attractive to international companies by cutting labour costs and offering inducements such as high guaranteed prices or allowing firms to pay no tax at all due to legal methods of evasion. In pursuit of these aims, supervisory and planning restrictions will be abolished and EU regulation challenged, if necessary through withdrawal of membership.

Again we can query the extent to which any national government can really be effective here. Living standards would have to be reduced to those in rural China in order to re-establish heavy industry in the United Kingdom. The strategy thus appears unworkable. Cutting regulation by withdrawing from the EU is at least as likely to discourage multinationals from coming to Britain as to encourage them, since they would find themselves outside the major world market.

In addition to access to the EU, Britain has a number of other characteristics that are attractive to firms. These include the relative absence of corruption; legal and political stability; good transport and other infrastructure; high educational levels, cultural and sport facilities and so on. These more enduring features of the national context have a stronger

DOI: 10.1057/9781137473059.0003

appeal for multinationals than short-term gains such as cheap labour and low taxes. Britain itself may be a major market for such companies' goods.

With the uncertainties about second-guessing what world economic actors would do in regard to British government policies, it is obviously unwise for national governments to be too confident (or pessimistic) about attracting them. Uncertainty is compounded by the fact that general economic conditions may be drastically influenced by international political events (such as sudden Russian hostility) or technical discoveries (e.g., more oil reserves, fracking, nuclear fusion).

Under these conditions steering the economy takes on a more exact analogy with steering a ship through stormy seas. What governments have claimed to do – but obviously failed – is to control the economic sea. To be absolutely sure the ship is safe, they aspire to calming the winds and smoothing the waves. Once this is done they claim they can steer the 'ship of state' through calm waters to its destination – well-being for all.

The only trouble is that governments have shown absolutely no sign of any ability to calm the surrounding sea. Any experienced sea captain will tell you that this cannot be done. What we can do, on the other hand, is to make sure the ship itself is in good order – well-overhauled, with an efficient and motivated crew and equipment necessary to confront the roughest waters, but also to make good speed in the calm that prevails most of the time.

In the rest of this book we will argue that national governments ought to concentrate on strengthening their ship and its crew – thus ensuring that they have the best chance of survival – rather than on calming the cruel and uncontrollable sea. Governments should concentrate in other words on what they can do politically, within their own territory, not on economic activities they can do little to influence given that they emanate from a global economy. Chapter 2 will support this argument by reviewing recent research findings on the nature of the global economy and Britain's place in it.

## Notes

1    These data are from the World Bank's World Development Indicators dataset at worldbank.org.

2   As the UK Treasury and the World Bank calculate GDP in slightly different
    ways, these calculations compare World Bank estimates of UK growth
    rates with World Bank data for the other states included here for the first
    set of coefficients; and UK Treasury predictions and UK Treasury reported
    outcomes for the final coefficient.

DOI: 10.1057/9781137473059.0003

# 2
# Globalization and Its Effects

Abstract: *Chapter 2 will present evidence to support the first plank in the argument: the nature of the global economy and the constraints it imposes on policy makers. The evolution of globalization will be traced over time and its implications and economic effects will be outlined. Evidence will be drawn from a variety of sources, including comparative political economy and official statistics.*

Keywords: economic governance; economic growth; global economy; globalization; UK economy

Budge, Ian with Sarah Birch. *National Policy in a Global Economy: How Government Can Improve Living Standards and Balance the Books.* Basingstoke: Palgrave Macmillan, 2014. DOI: 10.1057/9781137473059.0004.

This chapter will summarize evidence from the academic literature that supports the first plank in our argument: the nature of the global economy and the constraints it imposes on policy-makers. We will show that economic decision-making in the twenty-first century takes place in a context that differs radically from that assumed by traditional economic theory. This strongly suggests that the concept of national economies is obsolete, particularly in the United Kingdom. The forces that affect economic performance are mostly global in nature. UK policy-makers thus have very little scope to change things. Globalization is partly the result of policy decisions made by Westminster earlier on. But this does not alter the fact that economic developments in the United Kingdom are now inextricably intertwined with those taking place outside Britain's borders. It is impossible for policy-makers to turn the clock back, even were they so minded.

The chapter starts by reviewing the concept of globalization and tracing its evolution, before going on to review its principal economic effects on the United Kingdom and their implications for governance in the current context.

## The concept of globalization and its evolution

Globalization has been one of the most prominent topics in recent analyses of political economy, generating a voluminous academic literature and an equally large number of journalistic and popular analyses. However, different scholars use the term in different ways, so any discussion must be prefaced with a working definition that sets out clearly how the term will be employed here.

In a broad sense the world has been 'global' for centuries. Bronze Age communities actively traded goods across what are today national borders. And ever since Ferdinand Magellan's expedition first circumnavigated the globe in 1522, influences of various sorts have flowed across the whole of the earth (Woods, 2000: 2). Nevertheless, there has been a marked increase in the pace of globalization since the latter part of the nineteenth century, a trend which accelerated dramatically after the 1970s. This increase was fuelled by technological, social and political change.[1]

In the contemporary world globalization has several dimensions. One is political – the dense network of international regimes governing

DOI: 10.1057/9781137473059.0004

everything from the environment to crimes against humanity. People's cultural and social worlds have also been affected. Ideas, lifestyles and artistic trends spread almost instantaneously across the world. However, the aspect we focus on here is economic globalization – the dimension most commonly referenced when the term is employed. For our purposes, globalization will be defined as the increased inflows of goods and services, capital and people across national borders, and the rise in inter-state dependence that this engenders.

While our main concern is economic globalization, it is worth emphasizing that the different dimensions of globalization are intimately intertwined. Economic change is one of the principal drivers of political policy-making, both on domestic and international levels. Political decisions within economically influential states as well as within international organizations can have considerable impacts on the global economy. Two obvious examples are the under-regulation of financial products in the United States which sparked off the sub-prime mortgage crisis of 2008 and the steepest economic recession since the 1930s. OPEC's politically motivated decision to restrict the global supply of oil in the early 1970s, prompting the economic downturn of the mid-1970s, is another example of a decision by an international organization which had major global ramifications.

It is also clear that economic globalization affects social and cultural change the world over. The dissemination of new technologies and products alters the way people eat, work, maintain their health, provide shelter for themselves, communicate and relax. The advent of satellite television, the Internet and mobile telephony have also dramatically sped up the dissemination of ideas, behaviours and knowledge of successful strategies in all aspects of human endeavour. These behavioural changes have in turn impacted on both politics and the economy. It thus makes little sense conceptually to isolate one aspect of globalization from the phenomenon as a whole. For analytic purposes, however, our primary focus is on the implications of economic globalization for domestic policy-making.

The digital revolution and the deregulation of capital markets are the two recent changes most commonly cited as causes of the recent wave of globalization (Woods, 2000). The speed with which information can now be transmitted across the globe, and the unprecedented rise in the volume of information being recorded and disseminated, has vastly increased both the markets that firms can reach and the range

DOI: 10.1057/9781137473059.0004

of products they are able to market to consumers (both individuals and other businesses). At the same time, the relaxation of capital and exchange controls that took place in the 1980s and 1990s have greatly increased the global supply of credit and facilitated cross-border trade, a phenomenon which has been spurred by the lowering of trade barriers by most major economic actors.

The result has been a significant increase in both trade and cross-border investment, particularly among highly industrialized states. Though the economic recession has altered this pattern somewhat (especially when it comes to cross-border capital flows), and though regional trading blocs are taking on a greater role in the twenty-first century (*Economist*, 2013b; Tussie and Woods, 2000), the world is still considerably more globalized than it was half a century ago.

A smattering of data illustrates this point. The trade exposure – defined as exports plus imports as a proportion of GDP – of OECD countries increased from less than 50 per cent in 1960 to almost 70 per cent by the mid-1980s as average trade tariffs dropped from around 25 per cent to under 5 per cent (Garrett, 2000: 115). During the last years of the twentieth century and the first years of the twenty-first century, more states expanded trade. By 2013, the value of exported goods and services equalled 32 per cent of global GDP (*Economist*, 2013b). Worldwide capital flows averaged less than $1 trillion per year until the 1990s; they then increased by ten times between 1990 and 2007, when they peaked at $11 trillion (*Economist*, 2013b). Though the global economic downturn has caused capital flows to fall by about a third since then, the amount of money that crosses borders each year is still many times greater than it was a generation ago.

Behind the headline figures documenting quantitative change, there are also a number of important qualitative impacts that economic globalization has had on economies over this period. It is worth highlighting six such changes that are particularly relevant for our purposes: changes in economic structure, changes in trading patterns, changes in foreign direct investment (FDI), institutional changes, changes at the level of the firm and changes in inequality.

The rapid rise of the service sector in recent decades, made possible in large part by the so-called digital revolution, has led to a global rebalancing of economic activity away from the extractive industries and manufacturing. This change has a distinct geographic dimension. The 'knowledge economy', which has led the way in the

DOI: 10.1057/9781137473059.0004

expansion of the high-end service sector, has exhibited the steepest growth in the richer, more developed parts of the world. Manufacturing on the other hand has to a large extent shifted to poorer countries.

The second notable aspect of globalization is the rise in international trade. This trend has been beneficial in many ways, fuelling growth in several world regions. International trade has also been found to reduce corruption and political misconduct of various sorts (Ades and di Tella, 1999; Sandholtz and Gray, 2003) and in some contexts to lead to an improvement in labour practices (Mosley and Uno, 2007). However democratic accountability may have decreased. Transnational economic forces 'do little to deepen and much to undermine the accountability relationship between national governments and their citizens and exhibit only meagre mechanisms of accountability to the people whose economic – and even political – lives they increasingly govern' (Sperling, 2009: 23). This is because the so-called imperatives of the global economy are often used by leaders to justify decisions that are domestically unpopular. In many of the world's less developed states, leaders have little choice but to implement policies that are demanded by international lending organizations such as the International Monetary Fund and the World Bank.

Thirdly come the effects of the dramatic increase in foreign direct investment consequent upon rising globalization. There has been a change in the nature of large firms, which are increasingly built around an international network rather than a home-country headquarters. This is particularly true of companies that operate in the knowledge economy, increasingly important in today's world. In this context, states (and regions within states) with skilled labour forces and good infrastructure can attract large firms more easily. Countries such as the United Kingdom are now obliged to compete not only with other developed states but with China and India for investment, which puts a premium on proving an attractive environment for investors.

The fourth qualitative change is the rise of international institutions that play a role in regulating world economic affairs and the economic affairs of groups of states. The World Bank, the International Monetary Fund and the World Trade Organization are without a doubt the most important global economic institutions. From the UK perspective the regional institution of the European Union is a more important

DOI: 10.1057/9781137473059.0004

international body. Other regionally important bodies include the North American Free Trade Association (NAFTA) and Association of South-East Asian Nations (ASEAN). We cannot ignore the role of the international lending institutions in developed economies (indeed the United Kingdom was the first advanced industrialized state to have been bailed out by the IMF in 1976). But their role in globalization is considerably less marked in Europe than elsewhere.

A fifth aspect of globalization is the rise of multinational corporations. Some of them now have larger annual turnovers than many of the states in which they operate. At the turn of the twenty-first century, there were an estimated 78,000 transnational corporations in the world, and the annual sales of each of the six largest exceeded the GDP of all but 21 states. In 2002, the top 200 corporations had combined sales equivalent to 28 per cent of global GDP (Sikka, 2011). The advent of the knowledge-based economy and the speed with which services can be provided globally in the digital age have globalized markets in many spheres. At the same time, the end of the Cold War and the 'marketization' of virtually all former-communist states (as well as some states, such as China, which still describe themselves as 'communist') have also played important roles in expanding markets. Larger markets mean larger firms.

The sixth and final aspect of globalization that merits attention is the increase in global inequality, which has reached staggering proportions. A recent Oxfam report shows that half the world's wealth is owned by only 1 per cent of the global population (Oxfam, 2014a). Historic data demonstrate that world inequality was high in previous eras, with the global Gini coefficient of inequality approximating .50 at the start of the nineteenth century, rising to .61 at the start of the First World War and to .64 in the 1950s and .66 in the early 1990s (Bourguignon and Morrisson, 2002: 731–2). It is clear from these figures that though inequality is still rising, the greatest increases took place *before* the dramatic upswing in globalization which occurred in the 1970s. Since that time, inequality has risen more rapidly within countries than between them (734). The Oxfam report cited above shows that 70 per cent of the world's population live in states where inequality has increased in the past 30 years (Oxfam, 2014a). The increase in aggregate human wealth brought about by the rise in global economic interconnectedness over the past two centuries has not had the effect of lifting all up equally, though in theory

DOI: 10.1057/9781137473059.0004

it could have done so. Bourguignon and Morrisson (2002) demonstrate this with their careful analysis of the data:

> World economic growth since 1820 could have caused poverty to decline dramatically, despite population growth, had the world distribution of income remained unchanged-that is, had the growth rate of income been the same across and within countries. Had that been the case, the number of poor people would have been 650 million in 1992 rather than 2.8 billion and the number of extremely poor people 150 million instead of 1.3 billion. (733)

Globalization has spurred inequality for several reasons. The first has to do with the link between globalization and higher levels of unemployment. In richer states, labour is relatively expensive, so geographically agile global firms are likely to hire cheaper labour elsewhere. The large transnational corporations that characterize the contemporary global economy can also realize considerable economies of scale, thus reducing staffing needs. Moreover, large corporations have the ability to develop technological solutions to many tasks that would otherwise have been done manually. This leads to machines replacing human labour in many large organizations. Globalization also fuels inequality because anyone with a good idea has millions of customers in a globalized marketplace. Thus successful businesses make more out of their innovations than was possible in the past, generating a super-class of extremely wealthy people. The opening up of markets and the digital revolution have created considerable opportunities for the less-developed world in the new knowledge economy. At the same time new opportunities for generating profits have amplified the wealth of the richest, exacerbating both global levels of inequality and inequality within individual societies.

Finally, as Thomas Piketty (2014) demonstrates convincingly, the increasing differential between returns on capital investment and returns on labour in a globalized world enhances existing gaps between rich and poor. This effect is exacerbated when corporation tax is kept low and taxes on labour and consumption rise (Genschel and Schwarz, 2013).

All in all, it is clear from the evidence presented here that post-war globalization has had a profound impact on the way the world lives, works and makes decisions. Few members of the human race can be unaware that they live on a diverse planet, and almost all are attuned to the myriad economic, social and political forces from across the globe that shape the context in which they conduct their lives. Nowhere is this truer than in the United Kingdom.

DOI: 10.1057/9781137473059.0004

# Globalization and the UK economy

The British have for centuries been at the centre of efforts to globalize trade. Developments over the past 50 years have reinforced this tendency. As detailed in Chapter 1, Britain was the foremost global proponent of free trade in the nineteenth century. As Hirst and Thompson (2000: 353) note, 'Globalization was policy in the UK before the word was used in its current meanings'. The United Kingdom is one of the more globalized states on the planet – and considerably more globalized than the world's other major economies. A brief examination of relevant data illustrates this. Figure 2.1 charts the rise of economic globalization in the United Kingdom since 1970 using the widely cited KOF index of economic globalization.[2]

In comparative terms these figures are also illuminating. On the KOF index for 2014, the United Kingdom was 17th out of 207 states, placing it in the top 10 per cent. Thus both in global terms and in relation to similar states, the United Kingdom is at the top of the charts when it comes to international trade and dependence on international economic ties.

There are several reasons for this. As we have seen, historical factors play an important role. The European location of the British Isles also gives the United Kingdom another, more proximate set of international ties which is even more important for the United Kingdom in trade terms.

Decisions of successive recent governments to promote London as a financial centre and to support the financial sector of the economy

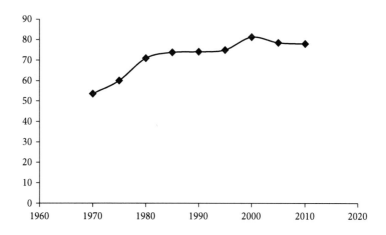

FIGURE 2.1    *Trade globalization in the United Kingdom since 1970*

DOI: 10.1057/9781137473059.0004

constitute an important additional factor. Most financial markets are global by definition. The strong reliance of the UK economy on this sector means that the needs of financial services enterprises loom large for policy-makers (Hutton, 1995). The UK economy is now considerably more globalized than other European economies of comparable size (e.g., France, Germany and Italy). No government could now do much to alter this state of affairs.

The United Kingdom's position in the world economy has a number of important implications. Summarizing a raft of recent research, we can identify three key impacts of economic globalization on the UK economy: increasing dependence on international trade, the shift from manufacturing to services and the increase in inequality.

Britain's rise as a great power came at the expense of its economic autonomy. Early industrialization involved specializing in manufactures and increasing dependence on the import of food and raw materials. This trend has continued in recent years, with the majority of trade now taking place with fellow European Union states. The United Kingdom is now highly reliant on other countries to produce the food that we eat and manufacture the objects that we buy. Perhaps a less obvious consequence is the United Kingdom's dependence on foreign direct investment to sustain its economy and employ its workforce (Hirst and Thompson, 2000). This dependence means that the United Kingdom is heavily exposed to economic shocks of foreign origin, as has been evident in the wake of the post-2008 economic downturn.

The past decades have been marked by the decline of UK manufacturing and rise of the service sector. In this respect, the United Kingdom is similar to many other developed states. One respect in which the UK economy differs from similar European economies is the importance of the financial sector, focused on London. This leads to both regional and sectoral imbalances within the United Kingdom. Hirst and Thompson (2000: 351) note that Westminster now has far less control over domestic economic processes: 'The effect of policy in the 1980s was to internationalize the economy further and cripple domestic sources of instability like the trade unions. Now the likely sources of instability in a very different economy are likely to be exogenous and uncontrollable international economic shocks.'

The third consequence of UK globalization is a substantial rise in inequality. Several recent studies have demonstrated the starkness of this phenomenon. An analysis of recent data from the office of National

DOI: 10.1057/9781137473059.0004

Statistics (ONS) shows that the richest 1 per cent of the UK population owns as much wealth as the poorest 55 per cent, and the top 10 per cent of the population owns 44 per cent of household wealth (Inman, 2014). A 2014 report by Oxfam shows that the five richest families in Britain have assets that exceed the combined assets of the poorest 20 per cent of the population. The incomes of the top 0.1 per cent of households have grown almost four times as fast as those the incomes of the bottom 90 per cent (Oxfam, 2014b). Many of those at the top of the ladder have been attracted to the United Kingdom by its permissive tax laws. Due to globalization, Britain has become strongly reliant on a system which perpetuates inequality. The heavy penetration of the United Kingdom by international business interests and the reliance of some of the most dynamic sectors of the economy (finance, property) on action by a small group of high-net-worth individuals have built wealth disparity – with all its attendant ills – into the fabric of economic activity in the United Kingdom.

Thus it makes little sense to talk of 'the UK economy'. Economic activity in the United Kingdom is so closely entangled in the European and global economies that a distinctive 'British' economic system simply does not exist. It might be possible to talk of economic systems in which entities based in the United Kingdom play a large role, such as the financial industry, or the global education industry. But this does not mean that these are distinctively British. Indeed, their success resides in the fact that they are global in scope, and the fact that an important part of these industries is based in the United Kingdom is a historical contingency.

## The implications of globalization for economic governance in the United Kingdom

The rapid acceleration of economic globalization over the course of the past several decades has had manifold implications for economic governance at the domestic level, above all in the United Kingdom. There is an objective and a subjective component to these effects as the way in which policy-makers perceive and understand globalization is as important for policy-making as globalization itself.

Objectively, globalization is believed by some analysts to place constraints on the decisions that political leaders can make. The most

DOI: 10.1057/9781137473059.0004

commonly cited is the increased mobility of capital in a globalized world. This has been argued to constrain the fiscal options available to policy-makers. Levying high taxes will supposedly drive multinational corporations to base their activities elsewhere. This effect of globalization has often been used by politicians as a way of justifying their refusal to increase taxes, despite rising deficits and inequality.

Yet there is considerable scepticism among economists as to whether high taxes really do drive away global capital.[3] There is only a weak link between the overall rate of taxation and indices of globalization such as FDI flows and financial openness in the highly industrialized states that are members of the OECD, though globalization does appear to shift the tax burden from capital on to labour and consumption (Bretschger and Hettich, 2002; Garrett, 1998, 2000; Genschel and Schwarz, 2013; Myles, 2000). Moreover, the fiscal policies of OECD states have actually become more heterogeneous since the 1960s as globalization has taken place. Political economists have argued that this is due to different states reacting in different ways to changing economic circumstances. Some governments responded to the deregulation of capital flows by seeking to keep both taxation and welfare spending to a minimum in order to attract international investment. But in most developed democracies, the dislocations occasioned by globalization (unemployment and job insecurity) have generated popular demands to increase welfare provision as a compensatory mechanism, resulting in greater public spending. On balance, an expansive response to globalization has been more common than austerity. Average levels of taxation and spending in OECD states have thus risen considerably since the 1970s, and they have risen in the United Kingdom also (Bretschger and Hettich, 2002; Cameron, 1978; Garrett, 1998, 2000; Rodrik, 1998). Thus globalization means that economies are buffeted by global economic forces over which they have little control, but there are multiple responses that policy-makers can take to this state of affairs. By no means are they constrained in the fiscal policies they adopt. Geoffrey Garrett (2000: 143) argues that 'if societies are to reap the benefits of globalization without paying the high costs of the past – in terms of social instability, nationalism and war – it is essential that governments ameliorate the unequalizing effects of markets. This is something democratic governments have always done and can continue to do even in a globalizing world economy'.

Moreover, there are a significant number of firms that have managed to do business in the United Kingdom without subjecting

DOI: 10.1057/9781137473059.0004

themselves to significant UK taxes. High-profile recent cases have included Amazon and Starbucks, which have been the target of a vibrant popular anti-tax-evasion campaign due to the fact that these firms have managed to trade in the United Kingdom while paying very low levels of tax. A variation in the rate of taxation would not affect such businesses to any great extent and would thus not risk causing them to cease operations in the United Kingdom. They are not based here in the first place, despite employing significant numbers of UK workers.

The point has also been made that service and retail businesses will go where the customers are; arguments about the mobility of capital have far greater relevance for the manufacturing sector than for many other sectors. Moreover, factors such the health and education of the workforce, rule of law and social stability – which are the results of relatively high tax rates – are often a far greater concern to multi-national corporations than the rate of taxation (Garrett, 1998, 2000; Garrett and Mitchell, 2001). Put differently, firms would prefer to pay the taxes that deliver these public goods, because the public goods are important for the viability of their business activities in the states where they operate.

Subjective constraints from globalization lie in the fact that policy-makers have different understandings of its impact, understandings that may or may not be accurate. To complicate matters further, democratic policy-makers also have to take into consideration the views of the voting public (or at least what they assume those views to be) on the impact of globalization and the viability of different policy options.

Many British policy-makers have over-estimated the effects of the so-called race to the bottom and the need to reduce taxes in order to retain business. Likewise, policy-makers often have an overly simplistic understanding of the way in which ordinary citizens attribute blame for economic outcomes (Vowles, 2015). There is evidence that in many developed democracies citizens (correctly) place a large measure of the blame (or credit) for economic performance on the global economy, rather than on decisions taken by the leaders they have elected (Hellwig and Samuels, 2007). This shift in blame attribution appears to have been relatively recent. But it has enabled political leaders in the United Kingdom to insulate themselves to a considerable extent from blame for the recent economic downturn.

DOI: 10.1057/9781137473059.0004

Witness repeated statements by both the government and Bank of England from 2011 to 2013 that their economic policy was being thwarted by the weak performance of the Eurozone. If they can credibly shift blame in this way British politicians need not be so fearful of the electoral consequences of their economic decisions. Likewise they are not likely to win many votes through seeking to engineer the economy. It is also worth pointing out that politicians can (and do) lead as well as follow public opinion. Research confirms their ability to shape citizens' understandings of economic realities (Pardos-Prado and Sagarzazu, 2013). Politicians can thus shape the public's view of what is possible for leaders to achieve and what is not.

## Conclusion

In this chapter we have seen that globalization affects virtually all aspects of society and the economy in contemporary Britain to such an extent that the very term 'UK economy' is obsolete. The United Kingdom is one of the world's most globalized countries. This may in part have been due to past decisions made by UK policy-makers. But now that the effects of these decisions have been embedded in the fabric of all our economic activity, they cannot easily be undone. Not only are domestic policy decisions no longer major causes of objective economic change. Voters also tend to look outside the United Kingdom to understand why the economy has gone up or down since the previous election. Leaders thus have little to fear from moving away from their usual single-minded focus on growth.

This new reality has profound consequences for the way politics is conducted. It shapes both the objective and the subjective landscape in which policy-making unfolds. Chapter 3 now considers how the developments sketched here impact in practice on what British governments can and cannot do in the twenty-first century.

## Notes

1    Globalization is often associated with the structural adjustment programmes that international lending institutions such as the World Bank and the International Monetary Fund require recipient states to undertake. But this

DOI: 10.1057/9781137473059.0004

phenomenon, strictly speaking, is not a necessary feature of globalization. It is also less relevant in the analysis of developed states such as the United Kingdom.

2   For full details of data and methodology, see the KOF website at http://globalization.kof.ethz.ch/. The data used here are taken from the 2013 release of this dataset.

3   See Genschel and Schwarz (2013) for a summary of this literature.

DOI: 10.1057/9781137473059.0004

# 3
# What National Governments Can and Can't Do Well

**Abstract:** *In this chapter the second main component of the argument will be laid out in detail: the real scope for decision-making enjoyed by contemporary governments. Analysis of the limits imposed by the forces of globalization will be counter-poised against an assessment of the room for practical action on the part of contemporary governments. The principal conclusion is that contemporary governments should seek above all to provide direct support to their citizens.*

Keywords: citizen wellbeing; economic governance; economic planning; economic uncertainty; government fiascos; limited intervention; United Kingdom

Budge, Ian with Sarah Birch. *National Policy in a Global Economy: How Government Can Improve Living Standards and Balance the Books.* Basingstoke: Palgrave Macmillan, 2014. DOI: 10.1057/9781137473059.0005.

DOI: 10.1057/9781137473059.0005

# Government and economy

Previous chapters have argued that national governments can do little to shape key aspects of economic performance, particularly in the short-term. This is because they are confronted not by a national unit but by a global one in which they are not major actors. The central players are not national governments but multinational businesses and corporations. In so far as economic activity in their own territory is concerned, governments may be the major employers and consumers. But they are far from dynamic entrepreneurs. The main changes and developments come from world technical and organizational changes or chance discoveries of natural resources like oil or shale. Even multinationals may not drive such developments though they often take advantage of them.

Examples of government passivity and inertia in the economic field are not far to seek. Wartime Britain produced the first computer – the famous code-breaking machine at Bletchley Park – and penicillin, the first generally available antibiotic. These were inventions which revolutionized the post-war world. In the case of the first computer the government broke up and buried the parts to preserve its secrets. The principles of its construction and operation were however applied by IBM (International Business Machines), an American corporation, to create a near-monopoly in the world market during the 1950s and 1960s. In the case of penicillin the government failed to take out patents on its manufacture but US firms did, building up a billion-dollar industry on that basis.

Belatedly the British government tried to create and subsidize a British computer industry in the 1960s, which failed. Major government efforts were devoted to propping up inefficient car production and shipbuilding in the 1970s. Over-reacting to these failures, the Thatcher governments of the 1980s sold off the old, service-providing state enterprises – power, water, public housing, which operated reasonably well – at knock-down prices, ultimately to multinationals headquartered outside Britain. Railways followed in the 1990s. The last bargain sales have been of the newly profitable Post Office and the efficient East Coast rail franchise in 2014, with the taxpayer taking over heavily indebted pension schemes to make them even more of a bargain.

The chance discovery of oil and gas in the North Sea had restored governments' financial standing by the end of the 1980s. This event was celebrated by deregulating banks and finance houses, leaving them free

DOI: 10.1057/9781137473059.0005

to speculate heavily abroad, to remove capital from Britain and from indigenous industry located there and to create immense risks for their customers when speculative investments went wrong. They did in 2008, precipitating a world financial collapse when public revenues and credit were called upon for colossal bail-outs in case the whole system collapsed and customers lost their deposits.

Perhaps in reaction to the failures of direct intervention (King and Crewe, 2013: 203–21), governments in the 1990s saw the solution as a handover of service provision to 'public-private initiatives'. In these projects, private firms, or a consortium of private firms, were contracted to take on some public work, from building schools and running prisons to reconstruction of the London Tube system. The companies involved were paid in terms of guaranteed future prices at higher than the market rate (a current example is the planned Hinkley Point Nuclear Power Station) or direct repayments from future revenues over the next 30–40 years. The arrangement was based on two assumptions: firstly that private firms would invariably do the job more efficiently than public agencies, and secondly that they would take over the risks involved in the project. Delays and overruns would cut into their profits without falling on the government itself.

Both assumptions proved wrong. With guaranteed returns, private enterprises had no inducement to cut costs or act efficiently. When mismanagement cut into returns they simply walked away (or threatened to terminate the project), transferring risk and compensatory payments to the government. The government could not leave a Tube line half under construction or a promised school building incomplete for the beginning of term, so had to offer more payments to the private partner or complete the project itself.

None of this is to say that state-run enterprises or services are inherently inefficient, or that governments do not have many successes to their name – the BBC and NHS, to name but two. Many local governments too have been very successful, and they are often accorded greater trust than their national counterparts (Allen and Birch, 2015: chapter 6).

The point is however that these successes were created for the non-economic benefits they produced rather than their revenues. Indeed many are publicly subsidized and might not be provided otherwise. Viewed in purely economic terms therefore, as profit-generating entrepreneurs, British governments' record is not good. There is of course no

DOI: 10.1057/9781137473059.0005

reason why it should be. That is not their essential role. As we shall argue in this chapter, the national government's real forte is providing for its population, a function for which profit-making is largely irrelevant and which should not be judged in strictly economic terms anyway.

If that is the case, national governments should not even try to act for purely economic reasons. Their actions may have economic effects but these should not be their driving motivations. Rather these should be firmly fixed on providing immediate services and benefits to their citizens.

# Forcing governments to be free: the paradox of policy-making under economic uncertainty

Given the uncertainties stemming from globalization and their own limitations as economic actors, how should national governments respond? Is there indeed any role left for them given the constraints they are now under, with the country's economic base in other hands?

To answer this question we need to look more closely at the nature of such constraints. In the British case at any rate they are nothing new and have in fact been present for 100 years. We saw in Chapters 1 and 2 how economic activity in Britain has been driven by world booms and busts – or wars – at least since the 1890s.

Government economic planning and direct economic interventions have been either ineffectual or mistaken. Where government has been successful is where it has ditched its economic preoccupations and provided direct protection and security for its citizens. Thus in 1936 it abandoned concerns about cutting public expenditures and producing a budget surplus to restore confidence in the markets. Instead it initiated re-armament in the face of Nazi aggression. Earlier, in 1912, it had introduced limited unemployment benefit, old age pensions and rudimentary public health services in the face of dire warnings about their effects on private economic activity – which its building of battleships was concurrently stimulating. From 1945 to 1951 the creation of the Welfare State and expansion of cultural activities saw citizens through a dire material crisis in the aftermath of war. There was austerity, but resources were spread widely enough round all citizens to provide for survival and even cultural enrichment through the public institutions.

DOI: 10.1057/9781137473059.0005

We can see from this history that the economic constraints have always been there – certainly for 100 years and probably longer. Globalization has always been with us, magnified by British institutional structures which leave finance and capital largely beyond anybody's control. Governments however have always been able to act constructively on behalf of all citizens to provide for their security (in the broadest sense) however tight 'objective' constraints have been. These have not been a real barrier to providing public benefits.

What *has* been a barrier are government's own ideological and psychological preoccupations, mainly focused on the (phantom) economy which exists in politicians' and economists' minds. Assertions that the economy would be crippled if spending on health and benefits exceeded even 1 per cent of GDP were the major driving force – or at any rate the major public justification – for opposition to the Liberal Social Insurance Bills of 1910–12. Cutting dole money was seen as the road to economic recovery in the 1920s and 1930s. Spending on life-enhancers such as education, sport and culture has been increasingly viewed as detracting from private 'wealth creation' and individual (economic) choice, despite considerable evidence from endogenous growth theorists that such spending is economically beneficial (e.g., Barro, 1991; Barro and Sala-i-Martin, 1995; Lucas, 1988; Romer, 1990).

Once the economic barriers to public action are seen as mere (but increasingly powerful) mental shibboleths, the way is clear to propounding the central argument of this book, which would otherwise seem paradoxical. That is, that recognizing their own economic powerlessness actually frees governments to provide essential benefits for their citizens rather than stopping them acting at all. As so often happens, the barriers to action are in political actors' own minds. So-called objective constraints cited as reasons for inaction simply melt away when put to the test. The most general is that public initiatives take away resources from wealth-creating activities which would ultimately benefit everybody more. There is little evidence for this. On the contrary aesthetic or military activities (to take ones furthest removed from everyday finance and economics) often stimulate economic activity (tourism, for example). Improbably, even obsolete military installations become tourist attractions, as do stately homes created for private pleasure and run by the (non-profit making) National Trust. We have already cited penicillin and computers as examples where economic payoffs were unanticipated.

DOI: 10.1057/9781137473059.0005

The World Wide Web is a more recent example of scientific endeavours producing huge economic payoffs.

Government failures to capitalize economically on such benefits – and almost infallibly to back declining industry and hopeless mega-projects like computerizing Patient Records for the NHS – just reinforce the idea that the government is qualified to act only to the minimum necessary in the economic field. This does not imply paying the private companies for vast developments with dubious benefits (King and Crewe, 2013: 195–200). If there are purely economic needs for new infrastructure, the private sector should surely be motivated to provide it themselves, subject to planning permission. Apart from regulating such projects on non-economic grounds, the government should refrain from meddling in commercial activity in order to free itself for its main function – responding to citizens' immediate and clearly expressed benefits and needs.

In the next section we show how such a stance admirably combines the basic precepts of ideologies which are generally taken as opposed – free market economics; neo-liberalism; ecological and environmental (Green) concerns; social democracy; Christian socialism; traditional Conservatism and populist demands. It does this by dispensing with their accretions such as Keynesian economics and narrow fiscal ortho-doxy and concentrating on their core concerns. We go into the details of this ideological reconciliation here. What it means in practical terms is that adherents of all the main party families in Britain and the world today can broadly agree on what has to be done. It is important that there should be broad agreement in a practical programme of action, since building a democratic majority is an essential part of the deal.

## What is to be done? Getting agreement

Governments should refrain from interventions justified only by their assumed economic effects and focus instead on providing immediate security and benefits for their citizens. That is the gist of our argument from the earlier part of this chapter and preceding ones. It divides into two propositions, negative and positive. The negative is to refrain from purely economic planning and intervention. This is what busi-ness spokesman, free marketeers and new-liberals have long argued.

DOI: 10.1057/9781137473059.0005

Governments are inept economic actors. So this part of the argument should be highly congenial to critics of 'big government'.

Governments, of course, did not come into being in order to trade or manufacture. They came to provide security, at first in the very narrow sense of basic physical security from dangers at home and abroad. Later however their responsibilities broadened to providing security against other threats – market disruption and natural disasters among them. In such areas governments seem well qualified to act – certainly no substitute has ever been found for them.

Of course actions in these areas have economic consequences, and often quite major ones. We have alluded to the role of pre-First and Second World War re-armament which was perhaps the major influence in ending the two major recessions of the twentieth century, after purely economic planning had failed. Providing for *social* security also has vast economic consequences but should not be judged primarily on these. Rather, action should be undertaken to safeguard the population's immediate health and well-being, and any economic consequences dealt with as they come along. They will probably differ from what is anticipated anyhow.

Such a policy stance is one traditionally favoured on the Left, but also by Christians, centrists and many others. It is indeed hard to argue against when stated directly. When it *is* opposed it is usually on the basis of extended economic arguments about whether it can be afforded in the long run, and bad effects on wealth creation which will solve everyone's problems eventually. The assumptions underlying such objections are often unconvincing, however.

It is here that Keynes's famous dictum becomes relevant – in the long run we will all be dead. Given pervasive economic uncertainty, extended theories about long-term consequences should always be discounted in favour of immediate benefits. Uncertainty and the fact that the assumptions behind economic interventions are often very tenuous are of course exactly the arguments we used in support of our first proposition, that governments should refrain from purely economic planning and intervention so far as possible. These conditions therefore – surely highly congenial to both sides of the ideological divide – underpin the whole of our argument. They lead inexorably to the central conclusion that Government action should in most areas aim for immediate, concrete benefits rather than long-term hypothetical ones, popular well-being

DOI: 10.1057/9781137473059.0005

now rather than economic gain later, whatever the proposal for getting there – either austerity or inflation, less or more regulation.

Of course these arguments apply in other areas too – (military) security and diplomacy, for example. Their immediate attraction, however, is their appeal to a variety of points of view about public policy, which are usually taken as opposing. If these can be reconciled in an immediate, shared, set of recommendations this could be very important for building a democratic majority to support them.

We can examine the extent of agreement by looking at Table 3.1. This goes into more detail about different political concerns and the degree to which they can be brought together in support of a relevant national policy stance.

What this summary table does is to identify the main clusters of political opinion which exist in Britain and most other contemporary democracies. Six are identified in the first column, starting with those who put an untrammelled free market at the centre of their concerns. Such groupings are often described, ideologically, as neo-liberals, as their views hark back to the free trade liberals of the mid-nineteenth century described in Chapter 1. Going on from these, Column 1 lists groups who feel that governments should take action to bring about various desirable objectives – the environment (ecologists and Greens): individual and family well-being (a traditional demand of Labour movements and social democratic parties, but also shared by Christians): the populist movements which sprung up in the hard times of 2012–13: but also, more surprisingly, by the kind of traditional conservatives found on one wing of the British Conservative Party, but who have lost influence there since Mrs. Thatcher's ascendency.

All of these political groupings agree on certain core beliefs, like the importance of a free market in the case of neo-liberals. But they also tend to have a more extreme element which extends their ideological views even further, for example, that free market relationships should predominate in all spheres of life and no other considerations should be allowed to stand in their way. It is these more extreme extensions of the doctrine which come into conflict with other points of view and cause them to be seen as inherently opposed to each other.

Actually as we can see from the policy beliefs listed in the first and second columns of Table 3.1 there is a lot of common ground between ideologies usually seen as opposed. Even the most distinctive position,

DOI: 10.1057/9781137473059.0005

TABLE 3.1  *How various political points of view contribute to a shared national policy stance*

| Political points of view | Derived recommendations which are: | | |
| --- | --- | --- | --- |
| | Important in Shaping a Common Policy Stance | Compatible with the Shared Policy Stance | Incompatible with any Shared Policy Stance |
| 1 Free market economics, neo-liberalism | Government should shed their policy 'overload' and only intervene in markets when strictly necessary and mainly for non-economic reasons (security, health etc). Unnecessary expenditures and regulations should be eliminated: budgets should be broadly balanced | Legal and democratic rights and freedoms secured by due process | Nothing should stand in the way of economic development and wealth creation. Private is always better than public |
| 2 'Green' environmentalism | Government should be prepared to intervene in any sphere of life (including economics) to preserve environment and other goods and benefits | Action should be undertaken by democratic means – persuasion, participation and debate. Voluntary action encouraged | 'Direct action' should be undertaken against 'bad' policy |
| 3 Social democracy | Governments should take whatever action is needed to secure the well-being of individual citizens and their families | Planning, regulation for largely non-economic ends | Non-emergency nationalization; Keynesian-style interventions in the macro-economy; very unbalanced budgets |
| 4 Christian democracy | Governments should intervene in any sphere of social life to protect the family, but not otherwise | Traditional morality should be advocated and strengthened through democratic processes (always respecting minority rights) | Imposition of any one moral or religious viewpoint |
| 5 Traditional conservatism | The first duty of government is social and individual security. Economic activities should not be allowed to disrupt long-standing social arrangements | Governments should provide families and individuals with a guaranteed minimum to secure their place in society | Government should be run by the major established stakeholders in society |
| 6 Recent populist movements | Ordinary people should be protected against adverse economic and social developments | Democracy should be strengthened to make Governments more responsive to people's needs | Scapegoating minorities and outsiders as threats to the majority population |

DOI: 10.1057/9781137473059.0005

that of the Free Marketeers who want a free market to be left to function on its own without excessive government interference, can be accommodated by the other groupings. Clearly all would recognize nowadays that free individual choice of goods and services balances their supply with demand more efficiently than other social mechanisms (centralized planning, for example). All should acknowledge therefore that free markets need to be at the heart of economic arrangements in a society and so strengthened and protected so far as possible. Indeed this is a traditional role of governments in our society. Free markets can often be undermined by monopolies and cartels which conspire to fix prices and artificially restrict supply. Such anti-competitive arrangements cannot be eliminated by the markets, which rely on governments to regulate them.

What the other opinion groupings listed in Table 3.1 cannot tolerate, however, is that market dealing should be allowed to override all other social values and arrangements. The countryside, for example, is more than just square units of land to be sold for commercial agriculture and housing. It has an aesthetic, cultural and environmental value of its own which sets limits on sale and purchase in free market terms. Similarly with family cohesion and public health. Wages cannot be beaten down by commercial forces to purely subsistence levels and left as the sole basis for family survival. Nor can we go back to the seventeenth-century situation where the free market in arms allowed Amsterdam dealers to equip the Spanish troops who were invading them from the south (though some might say the international arms trade is not too different today!).

Most groups, therefore – including neo-liberals – would argue that markets need to have limits set where other social values come in and are threatened by their operation. Where this is clearly the case governments need to set such limits. They should not in other words be operating as entrepreneurs or economic sponsors in the markets themselves. We have in fact argued above that they should move towards liquidating any such involvement. But when other values and social benefits are immediately involved then they should act, even if it means restricting market freedoms and choices or possibilities for wealth creation.

While most citizens and most groupings of opinion would agree with this position at a general level, the devil is always in the detail. Most political disputes involve fine judgements about what benefits exactly are at stake and whether they might be better enhanced by wealth from further economic development than by regulating and restricting it. It is here, however, that our caveat about weighting immediate and clear

DOI: 10.1057/9781137473059.0005

losses (or benefits) over long term and hypothetical ones comes in as a basis for deciding on government action. Long-term gains are generally calculated on the basis of controvertible projections and assumptions which are in danger of reversal should social and international trends go another way. The longer term they are the more they should be discounted. In the modern world, technological and environmental change, international relations and many other factors are likely to invalidate current extrapolations, and they should certainly be allowed to do so in government thinking.

There is nothing here to offend free market advocates. Indeed, one of our arguments in regard to economic developments in fields like transport and power is that they should be evaluated in terms of entrepreneurs' willingness to undertake initiatives with their own resources, if planning permission were granted on the social and environmental grounds mentioned earlier. We might in these areas give free enterprise more of a role than it has had in deciding whether projects and practices should go ahead. We can all agree that governments should never proceed with purely economic projects where private enterprise on its own would not do so.

One thing most strands of opinion agree on in Britain and democracies like it is that decisions should ultimately be made according to majority wishes. Only relatively extreme ideologues feel that their concerns are so important that they should be imposed on the rest of us without our consent. Our analysis and arguments here and in the rest of this book are designed to inform democratic discussion and hopefully guide it in certain directions but certainly not to pre-empt it.

To contribute usefully to detailed evaluation of particular lines of policy, however, we have to spell out our own discussion in greater detail. It is all very well saying in general that governments should give up trying to shape a non-existent British economy but rather adapt themselves to the surrounding economic as to the natural environment. But what does this imply for action in specific policy areas? We seek to flesh this out in the next chapter, going on in Chapter 5 to what is often the killer question, how can it all be paid for? Read on to find out!

DOI: 10.1057/9781137473059.0005

# 4
# Providing Citizen Support

Abstract: *This chapter will start where Chapter 3 ends, discussing in greater detail the forms of support which governments should seek to provide under the current circumstances. The main areas covered will be security, health, well-being, education, culture and democratic institutions.*

▶

Keywords: balanced budgets; democracy; public policy; public services; spending priorities; United Kingdom

Budge, Ian with Sarah Birch. *National Policy in a Global Economy: How Government Can Improve Living Standards and Balance the Books.* Basingstoke: Palgrave Macmillan, 2014. DOI: 10.1057/9781137473059.0006.

## Democracy as the way to find out policy needs

The most convincing definition of democracy has been provided by J.D. May and refined by Michael Saward (1998, 51: May 1978): democracy is a political system which ensures a 'necessary correspondence between acts of governance and the equally weighted felt interests of citizens with respect to these acts'. This is a rather precise spelling out of the general idea that democratic governments should generally respond to popular preferences. Indeed Saward suggests using the term 'responsive rule' as a shorthand for the longer definition.

However we cannot go on to shorthand before we clarify one or two essential points which are implied here. There is probably little dispute over everyone's interests being weighted equally – all citizens should count as one and none as more than one. Nor would most people deny that, apart from very recent arrivals, everyone living in a given territory should be given the opportunity of becoming a citizen. That implies that by and large policy should serve the interests of most of those living in the territory. Complications come in however when we ask what these interests are and how can we find out about them?

Over the past 100 years there has been a general move away from the idea that governing is such a complex matter that only a highly educated elite can really cope with it. In this perspective the rest of us can only judge occasionally whether results have turned out well, and even more occasionally whether the current lot of decision-makers should be replaced by another. From this point of view choosing governments is rather like choosing plumbers or lawyers – lacking their technical knowledge the only way we can judge them is by whether the water leakage continues or if we get the damages we are seeking.

The analogy breaks down however because, unless you are legally educated or have gone to plumbing courses yourself, educated and uneducated are in the same position with regard to technical experts. Having a general education is no guarantee that you are able to judge their work more effectively. Experts can contribute to general democratic debate just as easily as they can give advice behind closed doors.

All this adds up to saying that citizens are the best judges of their own interests, which are in turn reflected in their preferences for policy and – ultimately – their election votes. Voting in turn means that the general or aggregate interests of citizens as a whole are best reflected through the majority choice in an election, especially if that can be reversed in a later

DOI: 10.1057/9781137473059.0006

election, giving due time for reflection and actual experience with the consequences.

The fact that democratic procedures do make the election result and the majority choice determining satisfies the requirement for a 'necessary connection' between felt interests and policy in the general definition above. Of course there are lots of slippages and disconnections between votes and policies in actual working democracies. No one can really stand up and say the procedures work perfectly – though they obviously work better in some countries than in others. However if popular preferences, as expressed through votes, do not have some effect the country cannot really qualify as a democracy – which it clearly does in Britain.

## What do citizens feel they need?

By voting for a political party with a policy programme – all parties issue manifestos of the kind presented in Chapter 6 – citizens can indicate what they want to have done. But many other factors influence general election votes: the personal popularity of candidates, for example, competence; recent scandals; foreign crises. Besides, governments will often do things not covered in their manifesto or discussed in the election. There are lots of blockages, therefore, in the transmission of preferences into votes and votes into ultimate policy.

More specific information about people's policy preferences comes from polls and surveys. Being asked to express an instant opinion on matters you have only vaguely heard about also has its drawbacks of course and may well not reflect an individual's settled opinions. We will try to compensate for this here by asking more broadly what people want in general terms for satisfactory living and what government policy can do to advance their aspirations.

Not many surveys have phrased their questions at this broad a level. But those that have concur generally on the point that citizens are concerned much more with the substance and effects of policy rather than its form or the way it is delivered (Clarke et al., 2004, 2009). That is, unlike the political parties, ordinary people are not much interested in whether a service is public or private, outsourced or unsourced, or even foreign or British-owned. What interests them is its efficiency and reliability, that is, does it deliver what it is supposed to deliver, regularly and without fuss or extra effort. A further major concern is of course

DOI: 10.1057/9781137473059.0006

whether the services available cover the relevant needs. It is nice to have regular street cleaning but better if there is also regular repair and maintenance of the surfaces.

Concerns and political demands tend to be centred on the individual, but most of all on individuals in the context of the family. Personal security is of course always important, but more to be taken for granted in countries like Britain compared, say, to provisions for health. Schools are essentials for children but not only for general education; also for child minding and personal development leading on to social skills, entertainment and sport. Specialized institutions – parks, museums, libraries, the BBC – are important adjuncts in the socialization and education of children and adults but loom less large in most citizens' consciousness.

Here government responsibilities become diluted with voluntary and private provision. Jobs and employment, though the basis of family income and well-being, are primarily a matter for the individual and the market. The government here is one large employer among many, with no consistent preference found among the general population for private or public employment, each job opportunity being evaluated on its own mix of income and benefits.

The important thing of course is to *have* jobs and opportunities. The government is not expected to provide these directly. But it *is* expected to take action in any emergency, whether this is at individual level – inability to find work and therefore income – or in the face of mass unemployment (Whiteley et al., 2013). In both cases the first line of protection is of course income guarantees, currently provided in the shape of unemployment and other benefits. The question we have been considering is whether further action should be taken to provide jobs by regenerating the economy. Promises are often made to do this, currently and paradoxically by cutting the income of the unemployed in order to stimulate business. Plans of a Keynesian nature might try to achieve economic expansion by spending more, but usually not on personal or family benefits. We have been arguing that neither line of approach is likely to do much for income levels, as growing or stimulating the economy is something governments cannot effectively undertake in an age of globalization. Promises to do so can often be seen as ways of evading responsibility for providing adequate protection against economic effects for individuals and families.

Whatever the nature of its reaction the government is expected to protect citizens against obvious emergencies – providing security in the

DOI: 10.1057/9781137473059.0006

broadest sense against threats to life, property and well-being. The question of what the proper reaction to such emergencies should be is the essence of political debate and party differences. From a citizens' point of view it makes relatively little difference how emergency help is provided if it is effective; the same popular attitude that prevails generally in terms of all service provision by government.

This means that most citizens, electors and voters are not risk-takers. If current policies are providing adequate services and safeguards there is little appetite for new policies and safeguards (Clarke et al., 2004, 2009). Even a low level of provision may be jeopardized rather than improved by change. This explains why government proposals for change usually have more people against them than for them (Soroka and Wlezien, 2010): and why in 80 per cent of referendums in the world the status quo is chosen over proposals to change it (Le Duc, 2003). So much for those who see popular consultations as a dangerously radical extension of democracy. In fact those who have potentially most to lose by any change, in other words ordinary citizens, are most likely to vote against it.

If governments want to respond to the popular lead, therefore, they ought to be cautious and risk averse, in large as in small projects. That is a general orientation, along with the popular emphasis on effective delivery now as opposed to radical future 'improvement', which we carry over into our consideration of what national policy stance should underlie 'responsive governance' in a democracy faced by globalization.

# What national governments should generally do for their citizens

Caution and scepticism on the part of the population go well with our own analysis of the limits on what governments can do under globalization, particularly with regard to job and wealth creation. They cannot effectively direct the agglomeration of economic activities located in Britain nor greatly influence major decisions about expansion or contraction in the various economic sectors. Attempts to do so by tightening or relaxing the money supply or offering specific inducements like tax breaks, subsidies or specific bits of infrastructure almost invariably fail in their main objectives. Multinationals take what they are given but

DOI: 10.1057/9781137473059.0006

then move on (or out) depending on how they assess the situation in five or ten years' time.

Still more problematic are proposals to change already good systems – rail, motorways, telecommunications, electricity supply – which multinationals have already factored into their decisions. In their nation by nation comparisons marginal enhancements, even if expensive and disruptive, hardly count. Britain will be chosen as a location because of geographic centrality, good educational provision and infrastructure, reasonable security, political stability, relative lack of corruption and so on. Twenty minutes off long distance travel, back-up energy supply, the total elimination of Irish or Islamic terrorism or of street crime are hardly going to change the calculation. Such projects however are expensive and problematic from the citizens' and taxpayers' point of view. So they should only be undertaken if strictly necessary for internal reasons.

Generally, electors are less concerned about proposals for change the more remote they are from their everyday lives. This consideration helps to justify the reconsideration of spending priorities that we urge in the next chapter, as one way of paying for increased citizen support and services. What these should be we consider in the next section.

## What is to be done?

In facing up to the consequences of globalization for their citizens modern governments have generally followed two broad policy lines. The first, which has been reasonably successful in combating the most negative global effects, has been to provide various kinds of protection for individuals and families – against income loss from unemployment, for example; free health care and schools; organized cultural services and media; disaster relief.

The second broad reaction has been for governments to try to guide and expand economic activity on their territory. Economic expansion has occurred throughout the developed world and increasingly in the Third World. But it has been driven primarily by institutional and technological change rather than government action. For the reasons frequently cited earlier, economic developments on their territory are largely beyond national governments' control. Attempts to alter them so as to expand employment or attain other desirable goals are likely

DOI: 10.1057/9781137473059.0006

to be ineffective and wasteful. Public money would be better spent on individual and family protection.

We have argued, therefore, that the British part of the multinational economy can largely be left to the care of itself. If – as free marketers and neo-liberals have long argued – there is sufficient demand for industrial services or infrastructure, somebody will virtually always come along to provide them (at a price). The government and taxpayers do not need to subsidize large-scale economic projects. Government may well play a part in bringing potential providers and consumers together to discuss them, but it should not be paying for them. Nor need it subordinate all other social or environmental concerns to economic ones. Rather it should be aiming at a balance between them, while itself taking action in the non-economic areas.

We can identify five such areas where appropriate government action can significantly enhance general well-being. For purposes of argument, the various policy sectors can be separated out. In practice of course action taken in any one area spills over into the others. This is nowhere more evident than in the traditional responsibility of governments to provide personal security. In the modern world this has to be conceived in a very broad way taking on Tony Blair's (1994) pledge to tackle 'not just crime but the causes of crime'. General well-being from this perspective is an essential component of personal and internal security. So of course is foreign policy. If you oppose a United Ireland or invade Muslim countries you can anticipate an upsurge in internal terrorism by related groups, especially given globalization.

We shall discuss internal and external security mostly in the context of re-ordering government expenditures which we do in the next chapter. Our discussion here is focused on where the savings should be diverted *to*. From the point of view of general well-being and of citizens' own concerns the most important requirement is to have a guarantee of adequate income in emergencies. We are half-way to providing this under the current dispensation. However we currently do so through a variety of ad hoc arrangements and benefits which deprive those affected of choices (this should be of concern on the Right) and which fail to provide adequate support particularly for the worst-affected (this should worry the Left). An adequate personal income guarantee solves both these problems.

How could we pay for it? See the next chapter! Note however that we are not talking about universal shell-outs – covering those who have adequate incomes already. Rather we are talking about a universal public insurance policy, to be paid out only in case of need. That in itself should produce massive savings on current arrangements, quite apart from the administrative efficiencies involved in having one agency responsible for individual tax and (where necessary) income supplements. What is involved are supplements to whatever income one does earn, to bring the level up to what is necessary to live adequately and with dignity. Above that the guarantee could cover various levels proportional to what has been paid in contributions. To avoid the 'poverty trap' whereby taking on a paid job reduces or brings in no more than existing income, guarantees could be provided, perhaps on an individual basis, against losing out. Arbitration on such matters could be a new social service role. Or small jobs earning up to a limited level of remuneration could be exempted from consideration as in Germany.

Adequate incomes should not only provide better living all round. They should also reduce demand on, and under-pin, the more general public services which governments should concentrate on, starting with health. The National Health Service (NHS) needs to be made as comprehensive as it once was, with more of a focus on public health and preventive medicine that it has been able to provide under current cuts.

Boredom and inertia are as bad for health as more directly physical ailments. We have already pointed out that schools (along with colleges and universities) perform a variety of social functions, even if education and learning are at their core. These have traditionally been supported by governments because of their generally beneficial social effects – with individual (self-) improvement at their core. Quite simply the widening of our personal intellectual perspectives and skills and of our ability to appreciate, understand and to some extent shape our own environment, all make us better as individuals and as a society. This implies that education should be provided free for all who want to (and can be encouraged to) undertake it. It is not primarily an individual economic benefit providing a good job which has to be paid for.

Closely linked to education are culture and sport – the less structured areas of self-improvement, socialization and recreation. The social nature of institutions such as museums, clubs and societies renders them particularly important in strengthening family and social links. For these reasons they deserve as much government support as they can get.

Many cultural and sporting activities spill over into the physical environment whether built or natural – the settings in which societal,

DOI: 10.1057/9781137473059.0006

economic and political activities take place and which they affect. For the same reasons as with economics, the action which national governments can take in regard to wider environmental concerns is sharply defined and limited. Climate change, for example, is predominantly shaped by the actions of other players and any one national government has a limited say in the world arena. Still it has substantial scope for conservation at least within its own territory. As this has large and direct benefits for the relevant population it ought to be a major priority for national government action – perhaps the major area, along with personal income, where they can start to make an immediate difference to general well-being.

## Building majority and party support for revised priorities

Having outlined what should be the broad priorities for national governments, we will detail more specific lines of action in Chapters 6 and 7. An immediate question however is how the initiatives could get majority support given that popular reactions to government proposals are generally hostile (Soroka and Wlezien, 2010).

Even given popular majority support, a pertinent question is how such demands could be channelled and empowered in electoral and parliamentary terms? To this last question of course there is a classic and immediate answer – either convince an existing political party that it should take them up, or create a new one to push the programme. If there is any prospect of electoral success a new party is likely to form in order to reap it. UKIP (with rather different priorities) is only the latest example of a party being formed around a new programme in Britain. To facilitate this process in regard to our programme here, it is presented in the form of a party manifesto in Chapter 6. Party activity will go some way toward creating and organizing a relevant majority. But it will only go some way – one needs nascent plurality support before a party can really get going. Where is that to come from?

The policy priorities we have suggested match most individuals' aspirations for themselves and their families. What's not to like about proposals to guarantee adequate income and spend on public services directed to individual needs? The only off-putting aspect for the better off would be if they had to pay for them through increased individual

DOI: 10.1057/9781137473059.0006

taxation. That indeed is one of the traditional lines of division between Conservatives and Socialists, Right and Left. Given a situation in which they would have less and less control over what they had, due to higher taxation, the popular majority might well oppose enhanced personal provision – especially if they are taken in by specious government promises to grow the economy and increase wealth for all.

The solution clearly is to provide enhanced services and well-being without increasing taxes on individuals and families. Indeed it is hard to see how our proposals could be brought in without a general guarantee of a Pareto optimum in economic terms – that is, a guarantee that nobody will lose and many will gain from the proposed changes. How then could these be paid for? – while still maintaining the fiscal position; and broadly balancing budgets to meet popular desires for reasonable stability and an end to boom and bust?

We spell out answers in the next chapter. We propose a revision of priorities between policy areas – generally cutting provision in areas remote from the public in favour those which impinge on them directly. However this cannot pay for everything. The main revenue-raising proposals are to counter corporate tax evasion – by changing laws which permit it, if necessary – and to tax all economic activity on the national territory regardless of where ownership and control lie. National governments may be relatively powerless to influence multinational decisions about whether to locate or not in Britain. But this cuts both ways. If what the government does is relatively unimportant in global terms, the government is then free to act within its own territory on matters important to it – which include the policy areas listed earlier and the wherewithal to pay for them. How this can be done and the question of what reactions effective corporate taxation might provoke are considered in Chapter 5.

DOI: 10.1057/9781137473059.0006

# 5
# Paying for Support

Abstract: *The question that most readers will immediately ask is this: how can the support measures detailed in Chapter 4 be paid for? This chapter will address this issue head-on, setting out a variety of measures that will enable governments to fund support without increasing deficits or individual taxes.*

Keywords: equalizing business charges; government expenditure; public policy; taxing properly; United Kingdom

Budge, Ian with Sarah Birch. *National Policy in a Global Economy: How Government Can Improve Living Standards and Balance the Books.* Basingstoke: Palgrave Macmillan, 2014. DOI: 10.1057/9781137473059.0007.

The usual response to proposals for enhanced government provision for its citizens is this: how would you pay for it? This is indeed the killer question. Nobody likes their money and their personal freedom of choice being taken away. That is a detraction from individual freedom and well-being just as great as having essential services denied to you if you can't afford to pay for them.

When we talk about expanding public services and providing a universal income guarantee, therefore, we are not proposing to pay for them by increased individual or family taxation. Nor, when we talk later in this chapter about re-ordering priorities and cutting some areas of expenditure in favour of more immediate services, do we advocate the termination of existing contracts or compulsory redundancies. Doing so would run counter to the guarantee that no-one would be worse-off and many better off as a result of the proposed changes.

How then *do* we plan to pay? There are two obvious ways. The first is for government to reorder spending priorities and withdraw from some very expensive current and future commitments (High Speed Rail and associated preparations, for example). Some of the major areas of public expenditure are involved. So the savings and freed-up resources should be substantial.

Even so they are not enough to cover the even larger expenses of providing the enhanced citizen services and guarantees discussed in the last chapter. A new source of government revenue must clearly be found. That is the second element in our proposals on how to pay for proper citizen provision. This second element is simple but comprehensive – to tax all economic activities in the national territory effectively and on an equal basis – whether British or foreign owned, with headquarters, chief officer and legal domicile here or abroad. In practice, that would mean that multinationals such as Starbucks, Amazon or Nissan would be taxed on that part of their profits estimated to be made in Britain rather than leaving them untaxed through the legal loopholes currently existing.

These would need to be closed of course, which would involve an overhaul of the tax system and of some international agreements. The principle is simple and just however and difficult to argue against convincingly. Since similar British firms are less able to direct profits to tax havens abroad, it should generally benefit them. Consistent with the argument for governments not undertaking economic action for its own sake, the proposal is however a revenue-raising one to provide for

DOI: 10.1057/9781137473059.0007

individual services, not concealed protectionism. Any action government undertakes will have incidental social and economic effects. But that should not be its *raison d'être*.

## Principles of prioritizing

The first strategy in paying for citizen well-being is to revise government priorities in line with the general considerations put forward in the last chapter. In the first place governments should largely leave the economy to run itself and not intervene directly, except in emergencies. In particular it should not intervene or spend on long-term projects with vaguely defined goals. This covers a lot of construction projects such as High Speed rail and redundant aircraft carriers.

Where governments do not intervene directly they often provide special inducements to private constructors to pursue pet projects – house building or a 'National Energy Policy' designed to meet estimated future demands from British sources (regardless of whether they are foreign owned). In pursuit of this, consortia to build and operate nuclear power stations in Britain are to be offered hidden subsidies and guaranteed high prices for the lifetime of the plant. This is to compensate them for the risks which private enterprise would not take on if left to make its own judgements. Given the government's record of planning blunders it would be wise to respect business judgements in these areas and economize by doing so.

Foreign policy and military interventions are other areas where vastly expensive undertakings are pursued on the basis of vague and long-term 'strategic doctrines' and perceived threats which more often than not turn out not to exist. We consider these in more detail when we discuss security provisions in this chapter. Clearly personal security must be provided for citizens. But the idea of doing so by fighting wars half a world away rather than spending on policing at home needs more detailed examination which we provide here.

The general principle is however to centre spending priorities on individuals and families. So the more distant policies get from directly benefiting them, the more they should be scrutinized for unnecessary expense. This applies in particular to areas like energy (why not legislate to insulate homes and thus reduce demand?) foreign and military policy and their administration, as well as to the

DOI: 10.1057/9781137473059.0007

economy. All of these have been shaped more by ideological doctrine than by actual need.

This observation is also true for many services such as education and health which have been functioning satisfactorily but have been radically changed and changed again – usually in pursuit of mantras such as 'private good, public bad' (or the reverse in the 1970s, with wholesale change to comprehensive schools forced on reluctant communities). Another dogma has been the pursuit of 'economies of scale', which has left many organizations too large to manage effectively.

Given public support for current service provision, whatever its nature (if it is functioning reasonably) another cost-cutting principle of public administration should be to stick with current systems, unless their professionals and clients are themselves urging change.

Rather than embarking on direct and costly interventions which promise quick fixes, governments should tackle the roots of many current problems by regulation and legislation. This fulfils its major, supervisory role in society and economy better than plunging in as a direct participant. They also bring society up to date with technological developments which are capable of redefining problems and providing costless solutions.

A major example here is traffic congestion both on road and rail, round the big cities, above all London. Subsidizing travel and undertaking large construction projects like Crossrail (again London) simply aggravate the problems. When travel is made cheaper and easier more people travel. This subsidizes business in city centres by off-loading real costs on to the general public.

Meanwhile computerization has obviated the real need to travel by rendering it possible for most workers to do much of their work from home. The need to come to the office is for control not necessity. By legislating for a right of computerized workers to opt for a certain quota of home-based work, agreed by negotiation, commuting problems would be hugely eased and transport subsidies could be incrementally reduced without individual hardship.

This is but one example where lateral thinking enables government to reduce its own overload and resume its proper supervisory role, while reducing its expense. The cost lies in abandoning ideological blinkers. These condemn it to throw more and more money at problems without solving them and in many cases such as congestion simply aggravating them.

DOI: 10.1057/9781137473059.0007

# Cutting down big government

Getting back to legislation, regulation and supervision – the traditional roles of government – rather than direct and costly interventions (or even indirect intervention through market distorting subsidies) is one way of reducing government overload. There is however no getting away from the fact that government will always be the single largest economic actor and employer in the country. This is not to say that many useful and indeed essential services are not being provided. Public is not bad, especially where 'private' will not provide it – or if it does only for a few and/or at inflated cost.

Doing things for their own sake – such as providing for public health or the environment – inevitably has economic as well as social consequences. Government action should not be directed at economic effects but not held back by them either. What should be required from administration is that it should be done as efficiently as possible while not cost-cutting on its essential goals.

This might lead us in the first place to reconsider the allocation of service provision between central and local (and regional) government (or European, if British membership continues). The doctrine of subsidiarity – responsibilities being met at the appropriate level of government – has often been invoked to justify transfers of power from the European to the British level. It has been largely ignored, except by Scottish and Welsh nationalists, in regard to responsibilities inside Britain.

On the face of it local decision-makers are best placed to assess local needs. The argument against this is that it creates a 'post-code lottery' with quality of service dependent on where you live. This argument already seems to have been ceded however with regional governments having powers to structure and provide services in education, health, law, police (to name but some) which the Coalition government has abolished or changed. Where now is the argument for not letting local government do the same? Indeed one could go further, with Mrs. Thatcher, and argue that local governments should raise and spend their own revenue, and be held accountable for balancing services and taxes in their own area.

Unlike Mrs. Thatcher we should not confine the principle of local tax and spending to personal taxation. Like national government, local government should be able to charge all economic activities in their area. The practical difficulty here is the disparity in wealth and economic

DOI: 10.1057/9781137473059.0007

activity between different local areas, leaving poorer authorities less able to provide for their population. National government should be able to equalize here by:

a)   allowing for local taxation in its minimal income guarantee; and
b)   providing a grant to make up the gap between actual economic activity and average economic activity in the local area.

Promoting subsidiarity in this way should substantially reduce pressures on the central government apparatus. Central overload could be further reduced by taking advantage of the technological and communication developments cited earlier to disperse central administration and government over Britain. Cautious steps have been taken in this direction by locating tax collection in Glasgow, pensions in Newcastle and vehicle licensing in Cardiff where they all work perfectly well.

Why should dispersion, in an age of instant communication, be limited to relatively routine processing? Why should the major ministries not move out of London, an affluent and congested city, to less expensive locations around the country – reducing costs and increasing responsiveness? As the government is still the major economic actor within British territory, and has in this case control over its own decisions and their consequences, should it not disperse its economic activity so as to benefit the whole country – leaving London, as one of an elite band of global cities whose prosperity in the world economy is assured, to take care of itself. Parliament and Law Courts should also consider the move, possibly to Birmingham or to its depressed industrial belt.

Wringing one's hands over regional disparities is pure hypocrisy when political and administrative activity continue to be concentrated in London. This is perhaps the one area where national policy-makers have complete autonomy to make a major economic decision with immediate benefits. The same applies of course for Edinburgh as compared to Glasgow or Dundee, for the Scottish government, and Cardiff in regard to Swansea or North or Mid-Wales for the Welsh. The obstacles are all in decision-makers' minds. If they cannot make a contribution to regional regeneration in an area where they have control, how can they be expected to achieve it where they do not?

If European powers get transferred to Britain they should not leave congested Brussels for congested London. Technological advances also render it possible to bring home other overseas activities. Why should

DOI: 10.1057/9781137473059.0007

a network of ambassadors and embassies be maintained throughout the world, at considerable expense, when home personnel can get to most capitals in a brief period of time when necessary? Mostly however they can keep up with events from home through excellent press and monitoring services, telephone calls and conferences, and emails. Where a personal presence is required accommodation and office can be rented, rather than maintaining mansions and expensive homes. At least we should start with the presumption that ambassadorial letters and despatches belong to the nineteenth century, and experiment to see what difference they really make. None of this of course applies to the consular side of activities, which does social work for British citizens in trouble abroad and where a personal presence is probably required.

We go on to examine in detail the case for restructuring the way things are done now, in regard to security, both external and internal. Here it is worthwhile noting that an adequate minimum income guarantee will radically simplify administration by sweeping away the array of separate benefits currently paid on a variety of grounds, each of which needs checking and dispensing. What is currently paid out separately as pensions, social security, child allowance and disability and so on will simply be subsumed in the guarantee to top up income – where it falls short – to the level required to live adequately and with dignity. One financial administration dealing both with tax and payments can handle both.

It is certainly true that the Universal Benefit, introduced by the Coalition Government of 2010–15, was advertised as simplifying administration but signally failed to do so. This was largely because it was also designed to drive recipients onto ill-paid jobs through a draconian series of checks and delays in payment, actually increasing the administration required rather than reducing it. One need not anticipate a guaranteed minimum income encountering the same difficulty, calculated as it would be on income tax returns.

## Providing real security

To flesh out the general proposals for economizing on administration and cutting government overload – while paying for additional services – we examine one policy area in detail. This is security – which however encompasses a vast range of government activity from fighting abroad to

DOI: 10.1057/9781137473059.0007

policing and covers four major ministries – Foreign, Defence, Home and Justice – and major institutions such as army and police.

Personal security is of course a basic 'good' whose provision lies at the very origins of states and governments: their first and original function. Nobody is saying therefore that it can be dispensed with. It is indeed the ultimate foundation for all the other provisions government can make for citizens. However it need not necessarily continue to be provided in the inefficient way it is now. Cutting out the inessentials should free considerable resources both within the security area itself – for its more useful aspects such as policing – and also for other services such as the social support which tackles the causes of crime.

In the security area more than most, activities which seem relatively isolated from each other actually turn out to be closely interrelated. Much policing is in effect social work. Insofar as stealing and theft – and rioting – derive from poverty, underpinning an adequate income should reduce it.

In a globalized world moreover external action has a direct impact internally. The most obvious connection is between foreign intervention and internal terrorism. Refraining from foreign wars not only saves the direct expense but cuts out the vast expense involved in internal security operations against terrorism (not to mention dealing with refugees). We start our discussion therefore by considering foreign wars and the strategic defence doctrines which underlie them, and move on to the internal consequences and the expenses they entail. These are enormous so there is ample scope for cost-cutting to pay for more personally beneficial services, even if these ultimately require more money than can be provided by cost-cutting alone.

Our general proposition for cost-cutting on foreign and military policy is simple but far reaching. Britain should cease to regard itself as a global power and partner (even a junior one) with America in its role as world policeman. Rather it should take on those commitments associated with its real status as a medium-sized country in the North-West Atlantic and plan its defence requirements accordingly. Abandoning military and strategic pretensions parallels the renunciation of economic delusions about shaping and 'growing' activity in Britain independently of the rest of the world.

Actually Britain is in a better position militarily than it is economically. Nobody threatens the country. Its European neighbours are friendly and it is remote from the main trouble spots. As with the economy the

DOI: 10.1057/9781137473059.0007

solution is simply to refrain from invasion and intervention elsewhere, institutionalizing this decision by making intervention or war depend on a Parliamentary vote in favour – or even a referendum, since major public explanation and human cost is involved. Making it less easy for governments to intervene, and then shed responsibility to subsequent governments, is an essential part of avoiding expensive entanglements elsewhere.

Adopting a purely defensive role in the North-West Atlantic does not even involve renegotiating NATO (the North Atlantic Treaty Organisation), the American-led organization through which the United States has involved Britain in an inconclusive war in Iraq (2003–07) and an unsuccessful one in remote and strategically irrelevant Afghanistan. No other NATO member has felt called upon to act as the American spear-carrier. So it is diplomatically and militarily easy to opt out of the illusory Special Relationship, where only the burdens are special.

The direct annual costs of war over the past decade have been variously estimated at 4–40 billion pounds. The figure varies depending on whether only marginal or total costs are considered. Soldiers and aircraft have to be maintained and paid for anyway so the extra cost of sending them to war is not so great compared to the total budget. The main problem lies in maintaining an establishment capable of fighting widespread wars. Hence the need for a total rethink of Britain's foreign role and military posture in the first place.

Confining defence to the British Isles and their surrounding waters involves halving army numbers at least and giving more attention to the navy and air force. For greater efficiency the traditional distinctions between these should be abandoned and an integrated amphibious and airborne force created. Planning only for home operations, with support for UN peacekeeping, would in itself provide a barrier against expensive involvement elsewhere.

Two considerations interpose themselves when considering cuts to military expenditure. One is social and traditional in nature. The army in particular is not just a fighting machine but a social organization, dear both to those who have served in it and also to the mass of the population. The old regimental structure with its regional links is particularly favoured, though currently being phased out by successive governments in pursuit of the kind of integrated force mentioned earlier.

Given the traditional army's contribution to national ceremonial and tourism there is however no need to phase out the old structures – which

DOI: 10.1057/9781137473059.0007

could indeed take on a wider social role based on regiments but divorced from actual combat. That is, regimental institutions such as messes and appropriate buildings, with social and ceremonial functions, could be maintained as a focus for communal life and support for veterans. This is much needed as a way of providing a social context for returned soldiers, many traumatized or with physical disabilities who sorely need a relevant context and focus. The callous lack of long-term provision for ex-servicemen could be partly remedied by retaining these structures. They could in addition provide volunteers for numerous community and social structures and for additional help in national emergencies (particularly if they retained something of the old command structure). They would usefully add to the voluntary sector so important as a buffer against public service cuts.

One has to consider the domestic and social dimension of military reform. There is also the economic one. Perhaps the most important remaining sector of British manufacturing is the armaments industry. Integrated though it is into the global economy it has been somewhat insulated by a focus on keeping procurement national, and thus buying aircraft, guns and ships from national providers. Having a secure base at home, with enormous tolerance for cost overruns, has made firms highly competitive abroad. Cutting costs would inevitably have effects on their position.

There is of course a general question of whether British tax-payers should be subsidizing the overseas regimes which need military equipment. However the general response to an argument that particular sectors should be subsidized to preserve jobs must always be the same. Where proper social protection is in place, job losses no longer mean loss of income and status. It is surely more efficient anyway to pay the jobless directly rather than spend vast sums on an industry which is going under, in order to maintain the potentially jobless. Military procurement should provide the forces with the most appropriate equipment, not be used to keep up employment. Unfortunately that has often been the rationale for procurement spending in the past, as with other industrial sectors.

Intimately linked with procurement programmes is the vast and bureaucratic Ministry of Defence, notorious for cost overruns in the billions for electronics, missiles, vehicles and weapons, and inadequate support for fighting troops. To be fair, these are not entirely due to bureaucratic incompetence. They also stem from off-the-cuff political decisions on the one hand and long-term indecisiveness on the other,

DOI: 10.1057/9781137473059.0007

stemming from changes of government and consequent reversals of policy. The absence of a long-term plan contributes to these. So an irreversible downsizing to a purely regional presence in the world should help bring stability and reduce costs.

The ministry still stands however as the most potent symbol of government overload and the need for downsizing. Procurement and supply should be more in the hands of the military whom they so closely affect – within a fixed budget. Individuals at all levels should however be required to sign off items so that they can be held accountable for incompetence and waste and surcharged, as in local government. The ministry itself is too large and should be broken down into its constituent units.

As noted earlier decisions taken in one area of policy may impact centrally on another. This is nowhere truer than with external and internal security and the problem of terrorism. British foreign policy with regard to Ireland and the Muslim countries has provoked most post-war terrorism inside the country. While the engagement in Ireland could hardly have been avoided given the historical legacy, the interventions in Iraq and Afghanistan were avoidable and unnecessary, adding additional costs not only externally but in the creation of a vast and expensive surveillance apparatus.

Justification for its complete abolition comes from a comparison with Irish terrorism. Over 30 years this took around 3000 lives with substantial attacks and deaths spread over mainland Britain. Two nearly successful attempts were made to assassinate the whole British cabinet. A state of near war existed in Northern Ireland. The security response was largely to suspend jury trials in Northern Ireland while relying on normal judicial procedures on the mainland. Internment was quickly abandoned as a policy though special camps were run for 'political' prisoners.

In contrast Muslim terrorists have actually killed about 60 people at random in London. Action has been undertaken by small and disorganized groups or individuals and there is certainly nothing like the Army Command of the Provisional IRA behind them. Vague references are made to al Quae'da and international conspiracies. But none has really been pinned down.

Against this nebulous, limited threat an enormous and expensive security apparatus has been deployed at home and abroad, special legislation introduced and civil rights suspended. A whole radar installation (Flyingdales in Yorkshire) has been handed over to the United States

DOI: 10.1057/9781137473059.0007

while an entire secret coding operation of the size of a small University at Cheltenham works principally, again, for the Americans – but at British expense. What the 'War on Terror' declared by the United States has cost Britain is incalculable. But it is certainly enough to account for a sizeable chunk of the Budget deficit, currently financed by cuts to Health, Education, Local Government and family support and services.

Other indirect costs, from the growing alienation of immigrant groups to (inadequate) support for wounded and traumatized casualties of foreign campaigns, are also substantial. One paradox is that the billion-pound investment in harsh security measures, secret surveillance, foreign fighting has had little obvious effect other than to worsen the problem. The Middle East is currently collapsing in chaos, while a Russia which feels itself threatened by pervasive Western interventions has stoked up tension in Eastern Europe.

By a bitter paradox the few terrorist plots actually uncovered in Britain have been detected through ordinary policing, which is being cut to pay for flashier and costlier security measures! Proponents of these can always justify additional spending under all circumstances. The more plots are uncovered the more spending can be claimed to be needed. If none, more spending is clearly needed to uncover them! In an atmosphere of hysteria and fear both arguments have served to substantially increase budgets.

Our solution is to take no more action against Islamic terrorism than against Irish. Britain is fortunate that both are limited in terms of the British mainland. Security personnel should be transferred to social work and community policing, which are more effective measures against both political and day-to-day crime and anti-social behaviour.

Other heavy handed and costly measures can also be substituted by cheaper and more effective ones. A prison population now approaching 100,000 costs approximately £40,000 per person per year. Most prisoners should not be in prison anyway. The numbers necessitate a huge building programme which could be avoided first of all by substituting work camps for a drastically reduced prison population. Where violent prisoners need to be held to protect the general population, there seems little need to build superior accommodation for them. Whether working or learning they can be housed in simple conditions, possibly under canvas.

More important is to provide education for all, partly to improve attitudes and partly to provide simple skills like literacy which high proportions of convicts lack. Wherever possible however learning

DOI: 10.1057/9781137473059.0007

should be undertaken out of prison, in supervised environments with properly financed hostels and secure accommodation. With most crimes perpetrated by young males aged between 10 and 40, they should be encouraged into normal life beforehand, with the factors which turn most people from crime in middle age (stabler life style, family and children) fostered earlier.

Wherever possible punishment should be in the form of fines and income stoppages rather than prison. One simple measure is to require judges to state the public cost as well as the length of prison sentences rather than being invited to dispense them as though cost was not a concern. If each prisoner-year costs an estimated £40,000 the cumulative financial effects should be made known.

## Fiscal policy

Security is not the only area in which priorities can be revised and spending cuts made. Discussing it in detail however provides precedents and parallels for policy in other areas. It is not only a question of changing priorities between broad areas however but also of shifting priorities and spending within the area from counter-productive initiatives (wars, prisons) to more active social engagement (community policing and social provisions).

Changing policy therefore often directs spending elsewhere rather than just cutting expenditures – even if some savings will result overall given the money currently ploughed in to needless wars and worldwide, and domestic, spying. Our discussion shows how we can break out of this vicious circle where massive spending in one direction creates the need for massive spending in another.

Still, the savings are far from enough to finance the necessary protection from global ups and downs which we want to provide for individuals and families. This means that we must tackle the question of revenue-raising – without taking away in individuals' taxes what we propose to give them in services and income insurance.

We can only do this by tackling the question of corporate taxation head on – making it clear however that this does not involve businesses or firms which are not multinationals or banks.

Before coming to taxation itself however we ought to consider how much money the government could make simply by following ordinary

DOI: 10.1057/9781137473059.0007

business practice and charging properly for the services it provides. This does not simply cover general areas like transport infrastructure, security and an educated workforce but even more direct, commercial relationships.

The prime example which we pursue here is risk insurance for banks. Proper business charging here should however provoke a review of other transactions where the government provides business services which commercial firms charge for – special security and cleaning for late-night events, to take a micro-example. A thorough review of extra service delivery at all levels is surely required.

However the main sources of extra revenue are surely to be found in insurance and underwriting of risk. The government showed by its bailouts in 2008 that it would never allow a major bank to fail, to whatever extent failure was brought on by its own actions. Taxpayers, rather than shareholders or depositors, shelled out thousands of billions to prop up banks and keep them viable. On the basis of this guarantee banks have continued to take enormous risks on international financial markets, making equally large profits as a result. All banks, not just those with a nominal majority shareholding held by government – and even some foreign banks – can make gambles on the basis that if they are on balance successful, they can keep the winnings. If they cumulatively lose however, the government will step in and provide cash or guarantees to keep them viable to gamble and profit again.

Any commercial undertaking which undertook such a massive open-ended risk would be expected in the free-market to charge massively for it – perhaps to the extent of splitting the corporate profits. Yet the British government assumes the risk and the costs free – for all big banks it must be emphasized, not just those nominally nationalized where some returns might be expected from their sale.

Here then is an area where a consistent advocate of free markets would surely want their principles to be applied, with massive deficit reducing and revenue raising effects. Should banks then feel that chargeable risk-taking thereby became unprofitable and should be reduced – that would be an effect that governments have been trying to create ever since the financial crash. So it is difficult to see why they have not charged for the risk. The enhanced services which could be underwritten by risk-charging might then counteract to some extent the erosion of citizen savings caused by keeping interest rates low so banks do not have to pay depositors much for using them: 'quantitative easing' whereby the currency is

DOI: 10.1057/9781137473059.0007

depreciated by printing extra money to buy otherwise unsellable bonds from banks: and general cuts in services and citizen provision to finance the budget deficit produced by the banks' bailout in 2008.

Reducing the deficit is a worthy aim in an uncertain world, where governments should maintain the confidence of financial markets by balancing their books. That the present policy mix based on kindness to banks and austerity for citizens is incapable of doing so is shown by the increasing budget deficit of recent years. Less kindness to banks and realistic charging for risk are not on their own enough to close the deficit and tackle previous debt – particularly with the enhanced personal protection and public services we advocate. The only way to do so is to ensure that all who benefit also pay. To do so we return to our initial recommendation to tax all economic activity in the country, not just British-based firms. We consider how to do this in our next section.

## Bring in the multinationals!

Our simple but far-reaching proposal is to tax all economic activity in Britain on the same basis, whether foreign owned, domiciled abroad or registered overseas in a small country with a low rate of tax (many British dependencies among them). Such a move would not raise general tax rates at all. It would simply involve charging companies which do not pay proper taxes at the moment.

To do so would involve changing legislation and administrative structures to cope with multi-tiered companies with operations spread over many countries.

We clearly cannot go into intricate details here but the main contours of such a programme would be:

1  To change legislation to authorize such action and close legal loopholes which allow companies to conduct business in Britain and register receipts and profits abroad. One aspect of this would be to require companies to nominate a person or persons domiciled in Britain as responsible for paying due taxes here. These could be managers of the smallest branches responsible for taxes from their own unit, up to the director of the whole enterprise in Britain. These should be individually responsible to the extent that individuals in purely British domiciled and operated firms are.

DOI: 10.1057/9781137473059.0007

2    Such legislation would also require renegotiation of international treaties. To avoid long-drawn out negotiations, which were used to kick any prospect of realistic taxation into the long grass at the Group of Eight in 2012, their provisions would have to be temporarily suspended pending renegotiation. There would be foreign reactions to this. The potential benefits to other national governments from realistic taxation would be great however. So it is not clear how sharp reaction would be. It is also unclear whether Britain would be in the EU after a 2018 referendum on membership. So EU rules might well not apply at that time.

3    It is a fair bet that many multinationals might refuse co-operation, not opening their books or not disclosing total or British profits. Tax authorities would have to be given powers to operate on the basis of reasonable estimates, with a view to ultimately negotiating a realistic basis for taxation with the firm itself. As any payment would be additional revenue compared to the existing flow, authorities could afford to be generous.

4    We have already pointed out that multinationals have many more reasons for locating in Britain than rates of tax. In an unstable world the business framework offered here is particularly attractive. Comparable countries moreover are likely to bridge their own fiscal deficits by realistic taxation, following the British example.

Some businesses however are more mobile than others. Electronic-based mail order companies are the most likely to shift depots abroad while continuing to sell on the British market from their new base. With no physical assets in Britain the only way to counter such moves would be to block electronic access. Governments would have to be prepared to do so.

The consequences would be some loss of low paid jobs and higher prices for commodities like books and clothing. There are however plenty of rival enterprises supplying both. So if conflict continued such companies would simply lose out in a major market – and probably elsewhere. On the British side substitute companies would pay tax, so the state would not be the ultimate loser!

One need not however see the push to enforce greater transparency and ensure equality of tax payments as wholly negative for companies. The creation of hundreds of cash deposits in tax havens round the world also means that central management loses control and accountability (HSBC

DOI: 10.1057/9781137473059.0007

paid vast American fines for money laundering going on in accounts the chief executive had never heard of). Nor do business acquisitions driven by the need to use money reserves abroad rather than bring them under domestic taxation seem designed to increase efficiency through the market (Pfizer and Astra-Zeneca in 2014). Government regulation to avoid such distortions has long been recognized as necessary even by Liberal economists – particularly by Adam Smith who was far from being a Liberal in the modern sense. These are arguments which see equitable national taxation as more than a revenue raising device – though it is certainly that too.

Even in that sense however persistent national indebtedness is no benefit – indeed it is a threat – to international markets. Finding a stable long-term solution aids the free flow of trade and corrects the inefficiencies produced by the present imbalance of resources. For these reasons it has already found advocates from all ideological groupings. Once a national government takes the lead on its own territory it will find many more.

## A necessary reform

Staggering on from world financial crisis to sovereign debt crisis is no way to conduct a global economy. The root cause lies in governments' reluctance to act where they can – on their own territory – with financial prudence, while providing adequate protection for their citizens. Failure to do so leads to popular discontents which we have seen breaking out in populist movements alienated from mainstream politics and the global economy. Failure to act prudently on the fiscal side has led national governments – still the main political actors – into a vicious circle of service cuts and political instability. They can only get out of this in the long run by restoring services *and* fiscal stability. Trying to do so while leaving half of the national base untaxed makes it impossible to square this circle. But by bold action they can achieve this.

The solution lies in their territorial power if they can but use it. Hopefully Britain can take a lead here and again set an example to other national governments of how to deal with a globalized world.

DOI: 10.1057/9781137473059.0007

# 6

# Focusing on Action: A Model Manifesto

**Abstract:** *This chapter is written in the style of a political manifesto, with the aim of engaging the reader and developing a persuasive account of why our proposals make sense. It summarizes the demands of protest groups across Europe and the rest of the world, putting them in the British context.*

**Keywords:** Against Crisis Together; manifesto; policy programme; standing up for citizens; United Kingdom

Budge, Ian with Sarah Birch. *National Policy in a Global Economy: How Government Can Improve Living Standards and Balance the Books.* Basingstoke: Palgrave Macmillan, 2014. DOI: 10.1057/9781137473059.0008.

DOI: 10.1057/9781137473059.0008

In this chapter we change gears, switching from the abstract language of academic discourse to the way political programmes are usually presented – as an election manifesto for the general public. Its language is inevitably simpler and more direct – and often more fraught, never afraid of attributing responsibility and going into personalities. We write from the viewpoint of popular movements challenging the conventional thinking of the mainstream parties and the Coalition Government.

Putting things in this way gives readers a new insight into how our ideas work out as a practical programme, relating them more closely to current realities. It also fleshes them out, filling in details we haven't been able to comment on at a general level. Nothing we say here is inconsistent with our earlier arguments. Indeed it is a realization of them as a practical government programme for Britain in 2015. We hope some group may pick them up and run with them.

# ACT – Against Crisis Together

## A non-partisan programme putting ordinary individuals at the heart of things

▸ Against sham recoveries
▸ For new policies
▸ With immediate results
▸ Bringing benefits to all
▸ Giving real freedom of choice

# Crisis, recession and sham recovery – ACT's diagnosis

On the basis of another housing boom – which puts decent accommodation beyond ordinary folk – and increased sales (of imported goods!) the old parties ask us to back more cuts in public protection to 'finally get us out of the wood'. On the contrary we are just plunging back to where Gordon Brown claimed he had solved the problem. The Lib-Cons are just stoking another boom to win the election – a con indeed when they will cut health and welfare immediately after they win. Another recession will come, sooner rather than later. It is just a matter of

DOI: 10.1057/9781137473059.0008

waiting – as Osborne has waited for a world economic upturn to claim as his own.

Who is really suffering from the recessions which governments of all parties have brought upon us? Not big business and the banks. It is the ordinary individuals like us who are enduring unemployment, debts and cuts. Big banks have actually benefited from the mess, notching up unprecedented profits. Too big to fail they have been bailed out by ordinary taxpayers and small businesses – since they pay so little in tax themselves.

Why should we continue this way?

Surely it can't be the right. A sane society would be run so as to benefit everyone, not just those at the top. Family farms and entrepreneurs should be helped not exploited. They are the people who create the real wealth. Yet in the current ordering of things they get beaten down so supermarkets can outrace competitors to the bottom in terms of food, health and working conditions.

Why has this happened? Mainly because governments of all kinds have overreached themselves in terms of state interference and planning, crediting themselves with an infallible knowledge and control of events. In fact they have just demonstrated that they know nothing of what the economy will do (even next month) and excuse their failures by blaming other people or circumstances beyond their control – in the Eurozone, for example, which didn't recover quickly enough for the government's liking – but how it has boosted the British economy is never mentioned. Osborne and Clegg are just as bad as Miliband in thinking they can use austerity to produce their desired recovery. In fact the economy is out of control. All they have done with their grand plans for reducing the deficit is create general misery and chaos – far from the traditional Conservative and Liberal aims of a stable society and individual freedom. What freedom do we have from the banks and multinationals?

Our financial and economic crisis has in fact been matched by a political one as governments everywhere didn't tackle the real problems effectively. Their failure is also a failure of economic advisers who failed to spot the crisis coming and can't even tell us what will happen in six months' time. If they can't even get their short-term economic forecasts right, how can they tell us how to run society? Yet Osborne and his cronies want even more cuts and misery as the 'road to success'! Jam in five years or perhaps ten! – but scrapings today and next month and next year. Lacking any informed advice, government policy is now a knee-

DOI: 10.1057/9781137473059.0008

jerk reaction to financial markets – which they have managed to boost, temporarily at least. Bankers do well out of closures and bankruptcies followed by short-lived booms, but we don't.

Unfortunately the men pulling the strings (few women) want both cuts and growth – contradictory policies which impoverish and confuse citizens. That's where the old political parties want to leave us while they mishandle things at the top. They have no real answer to our ills. Closed-minded and rigid they just want to carry on in the same old way without any real consultation or debate which might shake them out of their blinkers. More cuts, slightly fewer cuts, reshuffle the NHS and schools faster or slower – they have no real alternatives to confusion, misery and pain.

Our plan does give an answer – Do what we can do politically – now – where we can really help people. This is not because of the far-fetched and long-term economic consequences such action might bring. We just don't know what these are. But we do know that expanding the NHS gives more people the care they need: adequate local services improve life in cities and villages and help small farmers to survive. By axing grandiose projects like High Speed Rail we can protect property-owners and our beautiful countryside and stop a rush of people moving into surrounding towns and villages which can't cope.

We can stop this destruction *now*, immediately we have some political power. This would also help us fight the massive tax evasion by multinational companies which would help us pay for better services and quality of life without increasing our debts like the government is doing.

These are only some examples of the immediate action we need to take to improve our lives. To do this we must first decide our own priorities rather than letting Miliband, Cameron and Clegg define them for us.

## ACT on priorities

Most people will agree with what we want to do. Basically they are the things governments of all parties wanted to provide in the good years of the 1950s and 1960s. After we define the priorities for political action we show how to pay for them by cutting unnecessary spending – as on the foreign wars most people oppose – and reforming business taxes. We want to make sure that nobody is worse off as a result of changes but many are better off – and things are also put on a better basis for the future. As for long-term economic effects, nobody can guarantee them.

DOI: 10.1057/9781137473059.0008

But neither can the unending cuts and misery proposed by governments and parties. Our proposals benefit everyone immediately – whatever happens with the economy. The first step in achieving our priorities is to define them. Here they are:

1  *Security.* The first job for the state is to provide order and security for individual citizens. Don't believe them when they say we can get this by cutting the police! It can only be done by strengthening the policing and emergency services in your neighbourhood. We can pay for this by withdrawing from expensive wars far away and spending the money at home, on the police and Armed Services in our own patch. Doing this will also help us to give long-owed support to the war victims – our own brave veterans who labour under horrific disabilities with little help from the swollen and bureaucratic Ministry of Defence.

2  *Health.* Disease and illness are silent killers which threaten us all. The only way to fight them is to make sure everyone has the best medical care. That can only happen if everyone is looked after by the NHS if they want to be. Cutting services and going for cheapness over quality is a strange way of providing this. It is a plan thought out by rich folk who are able to buy care for themselves.

3  *Well-being.* The foundation for good health is enough money to feed and house our families properly. For self-improvement through work, education, sport, culture, volunteering, everyone needs enough to manage with dignity and without anxiety. All citizens therefore should be guaranteed a basic income to cover old age and spells of misfortune and hardship. A universal entitlement to adequate income should replace the present ragbag of state payments – producing cuts in administrative costs and greater efficiency in reaching citizens in need. We can pay for it all by stopping unnecessary expenses like hopeless wars and useless construction projects and catching the big tax evaders.

4  *Education.* Education is the great investment we can make for future generations – and for improving our own. This is not just an economic benefit – even if it is the surest long-term way we can improve the future economy through better skills, self-confidence and knowledge. Education of all kinds – specialized, basic, general, training in skills or just acquiring knowledge – all make us better people, for ourselves and for others. Reducing educational opportunities diminishes us both as individuals and as a society.

DOI: 10.1057/9781137473059.0008

Current policies are cutting the branches we sit on – education at all levels should be free. An income guarantee will help many more take it up – and this will benefit everyone. For a better, more humane (and more interesting!) society we need to be able to educate ourselves at all times of life.

5 *Culture.* We educate people so they can share in a wider culture, whether technical, architectural, artistic, historical, musical – folk or pop, sporting, or carried by TV, theatre and film. Britain as a nation actually leads the world in all of these – but usually in spite of government rather than because of it. Instead of cutting support for arts, sport, community societies and clubs it should be increased. Talent should be encouraged and brought out, wherever it occurs. Instead of the shambles most football is in we should make sure that clubs belong to their supporters, not to greedy speculators who load them with debt. Sport should be a crusade, not a business. The same goes for all our cultural activities – nightschools, adult education – and broadcasting. The BBC is the envy of the world and has kept up standards in independent TV. But even this has deteriorated under government discrimination and vendettas while the media barons get away with their profits – power and profits being mostly what they care about.

6 *Land and people.* We live in our districts and communities, our cities, towns and countryside. Terrible things have happened to them all in the past 50 years. The full forces of commercialization have been unleashed by the EU, commercial chains, multinationals, developers and the uncaring forces of globalization. Families were promised homes which they now can't afford. Perfectly good houses stay empty till values rise. Whole streets and districts get demolished instead of renovated, because of centralized planning. Community protections are removed so developers can move in for a profit. Most of southern England is to be bricked over while houses in the North are left to rot. Small family farms are gobbled up by combines as prices for their products are forced down by supermarket barons. Sensible controls to safeguard our traditional way of life are weakened. The government not only sells off our heritage of woods but everything else it can, all in the name of cutting bureaucracy and creating construction jobs!

Most of these go to outside workers as in the Olympic development. Ask the East Enders what they got out of it except evictions and new

DOI: 10.1057/9781137473059.0008

commercial developments which don't benefit them. Clearly it's time to stand up for the small woman and man and for local decision-making, now restricted and cut to the bone.

How do we do this? The first thing is to guarantee everyone security through the minimum income guarantee. This will give everyone the basis for participating in their own communities which they need to do to defend themselves and make sensible laws for their own protection. We need to slow down or stop disruption and change. This is so often justified on the basis of creating jobs. Wrong. Incomers are recruited to work more cheaply and drive down wages. As for speeding economic growth grandiose projects to do this are just a con because nobody knows what the economy will look like in 10 or 20 years. One thing is sure: it won't be like today. The best example is the high speed railway through the Cotswolds, destroying the property and way of life of tens of thousands of people, nature reserves and beautiful landscapes – all to cut the train journey by 20 minutes! We need to get our priorities right – to slow down and take stock. Instead of subsidizing foreign giants to build more nuclear power stations – with taxpayers paying to clean up afterwards – we should put our money into house-insulation (which the government has just cut) using less power and distributing it better and giving local business a boost. Nobody should suffer from cold.

Conservation is also the best answer to extreme weather, which everyone knows is coming as icecaps melt and the seas rise. Globalization spreads new diseases – for trees, animals and people. These need to be controlled and combated. Governments have done absolutely nothing about this but sat back and let it happen. Half our trees are going: sheep and cattle are incubating diseases, and all the Coalition can do is cut research and let it rip. Probably nobody can get sensible international action to fight global plagues and epidemics. But that's no reason for doing nothing here and now to protect our own people and land.

## Politics and democracy

None of these good things are going to happen unless we open up ways to make them happen. We are not going to get action from the rich playboys (few girls!) who control our destinies in govern-ment and Parliament. The last thing they want is to have their gravy

DOI: 10.1057/9781137473059.0008

trains derailed, bringing down their high salaries and expenses and the chance of benefiting friends who can be useful to them afterwards.

There is little difference between mainstream parties on this. So we need to change the way politics is done – by letting the people in on it. Democracy means the people making laws and policy. The way to do this is by giving ourselves a vote when we want one rather than when the government permits us. Democracy is not a privilege to be doled out on a few special occasions. It should be the normal way of doing things. So let's not just vote on staying in the EU. Let's vote on going to war or staying out: on having good health services and a minimum income guarantee.

In fact, given the way governments have been chipping away at all of these, we need democracy not only to vote these policies in but to guarantee that they stay. If enough people want a referendum they should be able to get it through a popular initiative signed by a hundred thousand people. The results of referendums should be binding on the government and Parliament.

Making sure these do what the people want is also a problem. The parties were supposed to secure this by running for election on published programmes and putting them into effect if they got a majority. All of the establishment parties have cheated on this in the past ten years. Labour went to war in Iraq although most people opposed it. The Liberals and Conservatives cut the NHS and sold bits off after saying in the general election that it would be safe in their hands. They said nothing about selling off woods or starting new wars and interventions. Why couldn't they consult us?

Keeping decisions away from popular debate is helped by the secrecy which covers all of British government, particularly the Civil Service. If you don't know about decisions you can't influence them. So from the Cabinet to Cobra (state security) down to Communications (!) we have no inkling of what is discussed – except when it is selectively leaked by somebody who feels it is to their advantage or when it's revealed by courageous journalists. Channel 4 and the BBC are hated by parties and governments because they so often reveal what is going on.

But this is not enough. To really decide you have to know *all* that is going on, rather than relying on a few selective leaks. Nobody should say in secret what they would be ashamed to say in public. Freedom

DOI: 10.1057/9781137473059.0008

of information should not be doled out in small doses. It should apply everywhere. The Welsh government puts its cabinet minutes on the Internet. Scottish MPs do the same with expenses claims: eliminating the need for a special office to scrutinize and edit them. These practices work: so let's do the same in Britain as a whole.

Open discussion will be a great advance. Having decided what we want, though, we need to make it stick. The political parties are too shifty and tied to special interests to guarantee that they will pick policies for the general good. For that we need to have ACT in Parliament to keep an eye on them and push the public interest.

One of the things that can be discussed is whether the current way of electing MPs is best, since it gives the existing parties a cast iron guarantee of a seat in most constituencies. If we don't want to abandon our constituencies at least top up candidates should be elected in line with national voting shares. This works in Germany – and in Wales and Scotland. So why not in Westminster as well?

Before we can get any real change we need to get public-spirited citizens, fed up with the existing spoils system, elected to Parliament to keep the parties in line. So we need to organize and fight existing constituencies to get enough non-partisans into Parliament to stop special interest governments being formed.

A first priority is to work out how to do this in detail. There is nothing to stop citizens with clean records – even members of existing parties fed up with broken promises and harsh measures – putting their names down and starting to organize locally, using their own homes as a base if necessary. They face an uphill struggle against entrenched, well-funded party machines. But a big popular movement can succeed. By focusing purely on getting policies through they can avoid the perks and profits that have corrupted our existing MPs.

Where would they get their money from – and avoid being corrupted in their turn by the big payers? A first thing is to require our elected office holders to pay any salary over their guaranteed minimum income towards election expenses. That may not raise much but it will show that these representatives are not fat cats like the others.

For fighting elections they could rely on supporters' contributions with a limit on any one donation of £1,000 to make sure nobody buys undue influence. Mostly though they should base them on individual dedication and effort, exploiting new low-cost techniques like online and the Internet.

DOI: 10.1057/9781137473059.0008

# How do we pay for policies?

We've said how a new movement could pay to organize and fight elections. What about the cost of policies such as health, education and the minimal income guarantee? These will bring together a lot of existing public payments that are being made anyway, without the costs and bureaucracy they entail. For example, how much is being spent to administer and chase up student loans? Most will never be recovered. So the government is giving out money anyway but in a mean, cack-handed way that encourages waste and makes people feel bad about it.

Even though we operate more efficiently and spend existing money better, there's no denying that doing what we want to do for people will cost more money. Where do we find it? We don't have to be high level economists to see that we should broadly balance spending with income otherwise we'll run into trouble.

We mean to do this. But we have to discuss things in a crazy financial context where the Bank of England has printed £400 billion new notes and given them to the banks. The idea was that the banks would lend this to small British business, thus stimulating the economy. In the end of course they just sat on it and paid it out as tax-free profits.

In a world like this it's clear that paying for policies is not like paying in a shop, where if we produced our own money we would likely get arrested! We shouldn't defraud the public even if we could. So we should balance spending in one area with cuts in others or increased revenues.

Taking balanced cuts first. Usually when you hear about cuts these are to public services which help us all individually – in health and education, culture and policing. *We* should rather increase spending there and on teachers, police and fire services. The areas to cut are the wasteful ones like wars and the preparations for them, often involving grotesque over-spending of 1,000 or 2,000 per cent by the swollen and incompetent MoD. Punching at our real weight and concentrating on our security on the North East Atlantic would result in trillions of savings. By not invading other countries we stop stoking terrorism and concentrate on real security at home. Do we really need embassies with a big staff in 200 capitals throughout the world? Why don't we just keep a welfare officer to help citizens in trouble and fly out expensive diplomats to rented offices as and when we need them?

The cost of prisons is another example. Each prisoner costs £40,000 a year to keep – and there are 90,000 of them! Enormous numbers keep on coming back and no wonder with free board and lodging! We

DOI: 10.1057/9781137473059.0008

need to make crime less attractive by taking control of assets on arrest (to be released if not guilty) and vastly increasing police and probation services – stopping crime rather than mopping up afterwards. Supervised hostels, education and work – that is what ordinary offenders as opposed to fat cats need and that is what will stop them going back to crime. We need to rethink our whole approach to tackling the causes of crime so that law abiding citizens are really protected – not just throwing money at the problem by building ever more expensive prisons. What's wrong with tents and huts if the facilities for education and work are there?

Cuts even to the most expensive of these programmes will never pay for all of the benefits we intend to introduce. So we need to find new money to pay for them without increasing ordinary people's taxes. They certainly pay enough already. Our guarantee is that nobody will be worse off as a result of our changes. So everyone paying taxes now at ordinary levels can opt to stay with the existing system if they think they will be better off.

Where do we find the money – especially since previous governments have sold off public assets cheap or even given them away to donors and cronies? The answer is of course to change the tax laws to prevent non-payment especially by large corporations. Under existing laws paying taxes is entirely voluntary for anyone who can hire expert lawyers and accountants. Big companies – whether British or foreign – can set up offices in low tax countries and route their profits through them – paying nothing in taxes even though they make all their money here. They account for the massive decline in government income over the past five years.

They must be made to pay. Faced with popular anger the Coalition has made noises about tightening tax rules 'after getting international agreement'. Of course this means waiting until the cows come home and the people perish. The Coalition doesn't want to tax its friends and Labour has little appetite for it either.

Getting taxes from profits made in Britain is simple. We assess them if companies can't or won't provide their own figures and tax them here. Companies can then deduct the tax as an expense against profits wherever they do pay them. This is a simple and easy way of making sure companies pay adequately for the services they get from us other taxpayers.

Of course we can expect other countries to follow this lead and tax British companies operating abroad in the same way. That is only fair. It

DOI: 10.1057/9781137473059.0008

shouldn't affect our revenue much since big British companies evade our taxes just as much as foreign ones.

Will this make firms leave for lower tax countries? This is what the established parties say as an excuse for not doing anything at all. In fact the biggest offenders are mostly service providers and sellers like Starbucks and Amazon. They make some of their biggest sales in Britain. We are the open marketplace for the world to flood with their products. So multinationals are unlikely to leave in a hurry. If they do British firms will replace them – hopefully smaller ones which do pay their taxes, thus providing better local employment.

## ACT on the message

Don't believe those who say that getting a decent deal for everyone is impossible and we just have to suffer more misery until something turns up. There is certainly nothing any British government can do about the British economy (if there actually is one left and not just a set of foreign-owned subsidiaries). Because of the situation Labour and then the Coalition have allowed to develop, we depend economically on growth in the Eurozone or in the United States or China. Don't believe them when they announce bold new initiatives like High Speed Rail. All that does is put money in the pockets of big foreign owned construction companies and draws in more incomers.

Against this grim reality we have a message of hope. Help people because it's good to help them, not because there's a vague hope it will stimulate the economy. Our programme has just as much chance of doing this as any of the crumbling initiatives announced by governments with such fanfare – only to be forgotten in a year's time. But that's not the point. Rather we should take immediate action to get ourselves out of our problems because this will give immediate relief to individuals here and now – and we can achieve this now. So – reform tax rules, review public contracts, cut spending – all to pay for better health, education and welfare – not to mention sport, culture, recreation and entertainment.

Whether we get them depends on us and on our willingness to take political action.

We want a fresh start, not the tired old do-nothing politics.

ACT NOW AGAINST CRISIS – TOGETHER!

DOI: 10.1057/9781137473059.0008

# 7
# Putting Policies into Practice

*Abstract: This chapter provides an overview of the argument in accessible language, summarizing the main points developed in this volume and drawing out their practical implications for politics today.*

▶

*Keywords:* citizen good; consistency; feasibility; government programme; parties; political movements; prudent financial management; public policy; public services; United Kingdom

Budge, Ian with Sarah Birch. *National Policy in a Global Economy: How Government Can Improve Living Standards and Balance the Books.* Basingstoke: Palgrave Macmillan, 2014. DOI: 10.1057/9781137473059.0009.

An effective national response to globalization boils down essentially to two strategies: (1) Tax all national economic activity equally; (2) protect individuals directly against adverse economic and other developments.

These policies are intimately connected because equal business taxation is necessary to pay for protection. Implementing both policies is clearly within the power and capacity of national government. Neither unduly overloads it, since protection involves transferring payments to individuals to enable them to make their own choices: and in the broader spheres of health, education, culture and environment doing the same for organizations (from local governments to trusts and other voluntary groups) to provide services.

Of course all this requires checks on performance. But that is the traditional role of government anyway and does not require the massive bureaucratic apparatus needed to administer direct delivery. Clear individual and collective accountability and legal and regulatory provisions for pinning these down are much more important – and sadly lacking.

Compare such an effective yet minimalist response with the cloudy aspirations for 'economic growth' which governments put forward as 'policy' at present. Feel the difference! Such aspirations are usually used as excuses for failing to help citizens now – or indeed as reasons for worsening their conditions. We should cease trying to stop the tide of global change but instead run with it, while effectively helping folk threatened by it. Those coping well on their own should be left to get on with their lives.

# How feasible is it?

The manifesto presented in Chapter 6 provides practical proposals for doing so – which have in fact been foreshadowed in whole or part by many popular movements and new political parties over the last few years, from UKIP to Tax Uncut – or the Five Star Movement in Italy and elsewhere in Europe. In this concluding chapter we examine them from the viewpoint of feasibility and credibility. Do they stand any chance of being put into practice and if so how? Clearly they cannot be if they fail to hang together as an actionable programme. The first section of this chapter looks at their proposals from this point of view. If they are just a ragbag of unrelated demands, some of which are inconsistent with each

DOI: 10.1057/9781137473059.0009

other, they clearly couldn't be put into action at all. So they would fall at the first hurdle of providing a realizable programme.

A second essential for becoming the government programme is that they get enduring popular support. The emphasis is on 'enduring'. Any way you look at it there are too many well-heeled interests in the way of implementation. Mass rallies and demonstrations are important and necessary. But they will just fade away when chance economic upturns occur – and too easily disentangle (or are pulverized) under media and elite hostility.

This is because they lack an effective organizational base, such as the one provided by a political party. The movement supporting our proposals, as anticipated by the manifesto, might well be an anti-party party. But it has to have some kind of co-ordinating leadership – however democratic and responsive this might be – and a base organization which is capable of linking with and organizing the population. We look at this possibility in the second part of the chapter.

In conclusion we examine the prospects for such a national policy response being generally taken up and implemented. Besides stimulating its own support movement there is a slight possibility that a mainstream party might take up parts at least in its own programme – perhaps the British Liberals or parties like Pasok in Greece after election defeats in the next few years. In such a case (and after bitter experience) it would be necessary to avoid them dropping it after achieving some vote gains. The way to do this is to improve accountability both of individuals and the collective leadership. This could be enforced by direct democracy and control both inside parties and in the state as a whole. We discuss both possibilities at the end, before reiterating our central point – that both financial crises and sovereign debt crises are inevitable if national governments do not regulate multinational activity effectively on their own territory and use the proceeds to stabilize both their own situation and that of their citizens. In the next section we examine the internal coherence of suggestions for doing so made by the manifesto included in the last chapter.

# Popular alternatives to financial austerity: ragbag or unified rationale?

Popular protests against cuts to public services and other social provisions erupted across Mediterranean Europe in 2012 and 2013 and have

DOI: 10.1057/9781137473059.0009

been echoed in more moderate form by the North European Left. Movements like M5S put forward what look like a ragbag of demands – stop the cuts; stop expensive construction like high-speed rail; end corruption; care for the environment; extend political participation. We argue here that these demands require more of a coherent justification to make them stick, otherwise they will be defeated piecemeal, one by one, just as they have been made. Convincing potential supporters that there is indeed a strong theoretical and intellectual justification into which each of these demands fits is an important part of the current political battle. Most protest movements have not attempted this yet.

They need to do so because governments enforcing austerity *do* have a coherent theory behind them, in the shape of classical economics. Their argument is that to enhance financial confidence, the precondition for creating credit and thus stimulating economic growth, governments have to reduce their debts and deficits. Regrettably this means cutting welfare, education and public services generally. The long-term reward (they are a bit vague about *how* long term) is however renewed economic growth. By providing jobs this will do more for the population than state assistance can. However, since ordinary citizens are more concerned about their immediate well-being than jobs ten years down the line, the power to decide must be kept in the hands of the current political class who can be convinced, cajoled or coerced into taking a long-term view of the need for austerity.

To be fair, the established European Left opposes orthodox budget-cutting with a coherent argument of its own – Keynesian economics. By depressing economic activity budget cuts simply reduce growth and government revenue, thus perpetuating the deficit. The solution is to slow down cuts to services while spending more on large infrastructure projects and cheap credit. This will produce jobs now and provide a basis for future growth.

Popular protests have to counter both these reasoned arguments with a coherent set of alternative ideas. This is that globalization renders governments only marginal economic actors within their own territory. So there is little they can do to directly stimulate growth whether by cutting or spending. Government austerity in particular is largely irrelevant. What governments *can* do however is to act decisively to tackle the socio-political crisis produced by contemporary economics by extending services such as welfare and education. They should do this because these are good in themselves, rather than because of any

DOI: 10.1057/9781137473059.0009

imagined economic effects. Here we again fill in this argument for alternative policies, starting with the failures of economics and economists in the face of our contemporary global world. This makes direct *political* action by governments indispensable to protect their populations. It also brings together most of the demands of protest groups in a coherent rationale for such action.

# Globalization and the utter failure of conventional economics

The first step in any argument for political action unimpeded by fear of economic consequences must be to discredit the two theories which claim to be able to predict these: financial orthodoxy on the one hand and Keynesian demand management on the other. Discrediting these is easy because of the abject failure of their predictions over the past 30 years. Not only did economists fail to foresee the financial crisis of 2008, they have consistently failed to anticipate economic developments over the next three months! The reason for their failure can be found in the flawed basis of economic reasoning in the first place; and secondly in the development which has rendered this even more damaging to any analysis than in the past – globalization.

The basic problem of economic forecasting is – paradoxically – that it doesn't deal with economies! Instead it defines economies in purely political terms as countries and states. A territorial economy is not defined politically. It surely has to be taken as a contiguous cluster of businesses and enterprises which have more to do with each other than with other businesses across their boundaries.

In the nineteenth and early twentieth centuries as national territories were consolidated and internal transport systems improved by their governments (often for military reasons) there was probably a time when national economies existed as largely self-sufficient entities – probably never in Britain or the Netherlands but very likely in Germany, Italy and Spain. With globalization however autonomous national economies have largely ceased to exist. It is probably only the continental-sized economies – the United States (plus Canada and perhaps Mexico; China and India) – where internal transactions outweigh cross-border exchanges and where government action can affect economic functioning in the way Keynes envisaged. Possibly Germany with the Low Countries, Baltic

DOI: 10.1057/9781137473059.0009

Scandinavia, and Central Europe also forms an economy in this sense. However the EU and Britain clearly do not.

Economics as a discipline simply passes over this difficulty and assumes that contemporary states in some sense *are* self-contained economies. It is convenient to make this assumption because governments are the only bodies collecting economic statistics for territorial units. But it is fallacious to assume that this in itself is enough to create a controllable national economy.

True, governments are major economic actors within their own territories – perhaps the single most important actor. But this does not enable them to dictate the whole course of economic events there on their own. These days heavy spending by governments is more likely to suck in cheap foreign imports than to stimulate business within the state, while profits made there are channelled out by multinational corporations. Spending cuts cause immediate misery to citizens while doing little to reassure foreign bondholders and investors about the health of the tax base.

Globalization has abolished most national economies. But it has done more. It has shifted the structural economic balance between different areas of the world. As China and India acquire ever more sophisticated skills and technology to combine with their cheap labour and natural resources, areas like Western and Southern Europe will be less and less able to compete even on services and innovation, let alone manufactured goods. Governments cannot do anything to prevent this and are indeed best staying out of expensive, doomed, infrastructural and technological projects aimed at reversing economic decline. Investing in citizens' well-being and education is the limit of what they should do. The more adaptable individuals are, the better they will be in working with the global economy. Governments with their failed mega projects are not.

## What else can be done?

Social and political crises are hardly likely to reassure government investors and bondholders either. So a first task of governments, as it always has been, is to stabilize the political situation. This requires them to conciliate opposition by actually taking their proposals seriously! They should accept their policies not only to disarm a potentially crippling internal opposition but also because they represent exactly the policies

DOI: 10.1057/9781137473059.0009

which are within their power to pursue – and which they *should* be pursuing to provide immediate benefits to citizens.

This requires that cuts to services be restored and additional money spent on them. However spending on services does not imply a full scale neo-Keynesian reaction – massive expenditures without balancing deductions elsewhere. It is only prudent to roughly balance the books, as opposed to undue austerity on one side and irresponsible extravagance on the other.

How can this be done? Protest movements have already suggested one way, by cancelling dubious projects like British and Italian High-Speed Rail and the British nuclear weapons programme. Wars and foreign interventions should be stopped. Such expenditure cuts have not even been considered as part of the austerity drive which has focused on social and personal services. They should however provide some immediate savings. On the other hand it must be a principle behind all government policies that no tax paying citizen should be worse off as a result of reforms and many should be better off. Such a guarantee is necessary to generate general public support. So cuts or down-scaling in government departments should be by natural wastage or transfers of personnel to more useful activities elsewhere.

This means that administrative reforms will produce long-term rather than immediate fiscal returns. Another change which should be undertaken for purely ethical reasons will also produce subsidiary economic benefits. That is, requiring that all imported goods and services meet the same health and safety and labour regulations which each country's own enterprises operate under. This should include inspection to the same standards as in the country concerned.

Such measures could be taken as disguised economic protection, designed to safeguard home industries against cheaper foreign competition. Actually however it puts international trade on the same footing as internal trade. If we think it is necessary to have national rules to protect our own citizens, should we not apply them to protect South-East Asians or Latin Americans – taking into account varying costs of living so poorer countries can still compete on the basis of genuinely cheaper labour. We might also think of extending such rules to environmental protection. If we do not think natural degradation is right at home why should we tolerate it abroad?

Such measures would have the merit of putting international trade on the same basis as that at home. The decision to import dirt-cheap goods

DOI: 10.1057/9781137473059.0009

and so depress local industry and agriculture working under laws which we think are ethically justified is a political decision made by national governments or the EU. It should be discussed as such not disguised as economic inevitability.

Of course such decisions do have economic consequences in aiding local industry and augmenting the national government's tax base. They would hardly solve their fiscal crisis however and should not be undertaken to do so. Sovereign debt and fiscal deficits are in essence outcrops from this underlying problem. Governments are not raising enough money to pay for services they are morally obliged to provide for their citizens. How can they do so? How can they balance the books, which would remain unbalanced even if the suggestions made above were fully implemented. The answer lies in consolidating their tax base in two ways, while leaving individual tax-payers unaffected. The first way has already been suggested by Grillo and M5S – tackling the massive personal and corporate tax evasion which exists across Southern and Eastern Europe. This can only be done by transferring the power of assessment to the fiscal civil servants, enforcing payments even if judicial appeals are in process. All calculations and figures should be published on the Internet so that everyone involved including officials can be kept accountable.

In countries where corruption and outright evasion are not so much of a problem governments still lose massive amounts of revenue through legal, mainly corporate, tax avoidance. In essence multinationals and rich individuals create fictitious domiciles in low tax countries and outright tax havens. This is bad for the companies themselves – with 500 deposits throughout the world and opaque transfers many do not know what they are doing themselves, often laundering criminal revenues. But it is even worse for national governments who find revenue from their own territory diminishing and cut spending as a result.

This is however entirely their own doing. All they have to do is tax multinationals as they do national companies, on the basis of the profits earned in their territory. Where companies refuse to provide their own figures they can be simply assessed by taking local economic activity as a proportion of their total activity and taxing declared profits in proportion to that. Again the revenue raised should go to governments during any appeal in progress, any final adjustments to be made at the end. Total transparency on both sides should be enforced by publication and scrutiny on the internet.

DOI: 10.1057/9781137473059.0009

Any such national action to secure a proper tax return would of course invoke international complications and reactions. These could be met by the argument that foreign companies are being treated in exactly the same basis as national ones. It is a fair bet that many other countries would immediately follow the pioneer that made the breakthrough, creating an irresistible force at international level and blunting the argument that companies would transfer their activity elsewhere.

A further refinement would be to put companies on a monthly tax-paying basis to avoid government revenue drying up at particular times of the year and avoiding unnecessary borrowing.

# Conclusion: governments should act now to help their own citizens

This all goes to demonstrate that there is a coherent underpinning for protest movements' political demands which goes far beyond the simple restoration of public services and social provisions. On the one hand governments fallaciously see themselves as major dynamic forces, able to restore health and growth to a non-existent national economy. On the other, they refuse to undertake the necessary political actions by which they could at least restore *themselves* to fiscal health and finance their services to the population. The choice is theirs. Either they can negotiate with their internal opposition to produce a reasonable social outcome. Or they can continue to drift, blaming external events, the EU, Germany or immigration for their current ills and refusing to do anything about them – meanwhile waiting for an upturn.

But they can't go on like this for ever as it becomes increasingly obvious that this attitude feeds a general cynicism about the mainstream parties. In turn this gives protest movements an opportunity to change the current economic drifting into a considered national response to globalization. They should start reform efforts now by publicizing their agreements among the general population, lobbying the Opposition – and if they get no response starting their own new movement, utilizing devices like the Internet and Twitter. They can already base themselves intellectually on the Manifesto and programme outlined in the last chapter.

DOI: 10.1057/9781137473059.0009

# Getting support for alternative policies

In the Winter of Discontent (2012–13) a lot of protest movements sprang up, mostly advocating direct protests against the public austerity imposed to finance private bailouts. Wall Street and the City of London were occupied: Tax Uncut invaded supermarkets: protest parties both of the Right and Left got support across Europe. Most spectacularly M5S led by Beppe Grillo became a major player in the Italian Parliament. There is no doubt therefore that there is much potential popular support for the proposals we have put forward for a permanent end to fiscal crises of the type we have been experiencing – and to the social crisis resulting from lowered living standards and public service cuts.

Sporadic sit-ins and occupations, or strikes and riots, are not ways to gain lasting support however. They may indeed put people off rather than bring them in. It is focused, disciplined, lasting, advocacy that will bring in votes, particularly with a coherent and if possible fairly direct focus of action. UKIP in Britain and the Front National in France have found one by blaming the EU and its free movement of labour for all our current ills. Globalization will continue regardless of what Britain and France do to escape its consequences. Rather like hurricanes and surges sweeping in from the Atlantic governments should adapt to them – in part by providing safety nets and lifelines for their citizens.

Grillo's M5S movement had some inkling of this but failed to draw lessons about the organization and disciplined effort required to turn their proposals into national policy. The only way to do so is to convert or form a proper political party to contest elections and build cohesive voting support.

What prospect is there for this? Not great but not hopeless either. Greens and Left Socialists have plodded along for a long time building support for similar proposals. They are increasing their vote but possibly another crisis is necessary (and not unlikely!) to make them significant players.

Another type of protest party has made significant headway in its own areas. These are the minority nationalists like the SNP (Scottish National Party), channelling regional resentment against economic integration accompanied by exclusion from the metropolitan centres of power. Unfortunately their mistaken beliefs about growing the economy echo those of the mainstream British parties – it is just that

DOI: 10.1057/9781137473059.0009

they want to apply them at home – and would do so with a similar lack of success.

However the facts that there *are* new protest parties and that their collective support is growing do indicate the potential for change. Threatened by a loss of votes, even one of the mainstream parties might tune in to the right message in an effort to re-establish itself.

Mainstream parties and current media debate are not in fact wholly immunized against the need for realistic policies in an increasingly global world. The G8 Summit of 2012 supported action against tax havens – even though they promptly kicked it into the long grass by stressing the necessity of getting general international agreement. Negotiations of course never started though we would no doubt be told they are 'under consideration' – till the next crisis?

The only effective way to tax equally is at the national level. In this regard it is interesting that the *Economist* – voice of the neo-Liberal Establishment – has discussed changes in national taxation which would increase tax on capital compared to labour (*Economist*, 2013c).

The more such discussion spreads throughout the media, the more credible and feasible our taxation proposals seem. British dependencies (Man, Jersey, the Cayman Islands) are among the more numerous and prominent tax havens in the world. As usual the British government has the power to take action but lacks the will (Sikka, 2010). All that has been done in the aftermath of the 2012 G8 summit discussion of this topic was to impose a little more accounting transparency (accounts are still very opaque however).

Populists of all persuasions often argue for more direct democracy as a way of getting sensible policy proposals through. Give decision-making powers directly to the people in the shape of referendums (or even better, initiatives where proposals with enough signatures are automatically voted on). Corrupt intermediaries like parties and interest groups will be swept away. The people will then surely approve proposals directed at their own betterment.

This is an attractive vision and there may be some truth in it, given the guarantees against anyone losing out (and many benefiting) if our suggestions are voted through.

Experience shows however that parties, or party-like movements, are necessary to formulate proposals for voters, provide informative debate, identify hidden interests trying to table good-looking but wrecking amendments: mobilize voters: translate general directives into detailed

DOI: 10.1057/9781137473059.0009

government action – and so on, through a whole range of contingencies which do not emerge at first sight. Just as Parliamentary debate needs rules and structures to be carried on properly, so do popular consultations (Budge, 1996).

We are back with the unavoidable need for a party, by whatever name, to pick up these proposals and organize action around them. This may not happen immediately. Time and events are on their side however as world financial crises become increasingly common in the face of governments and unregulated banks lurching into vast debts and cutting citizen support. The preconditions for popular reform movements are all there. Let us hope they are directed to the constructive if drastic reforms recommended here, rather than riots and revolution. Hopefully, this book may help in a small way by providing a realistic diagnosis of the effects of globalization and a clear action plan for national governments.

DOI: 10.1057/9781137473059.0009

# Bibliography

Ades, Alberto and Rafael Di Tella (1999), 'Rents, Competition and Corruption', *American Economic Review* 89.4, 982–93.

Allen, Nicholas and Sarah Birch (2015), *Ethics and Integrity in British Politics: How Citizens Judge their Politicians' Conduct, and Why it Matters*, Cambridge: Cambridge University Press.

Anderson, James E. and Eric van Wincoop (2004), 'Trade Costs', Working Paper 10480, NBER Working Paper Series, National Bureau of Economic Research.

Barro, Robert (1991), 'Economic Growth in a Cross-Section of Countries', *Quarterly Journal of Economics* 106, 407–33.

Barro, Robert and Xavier Sala-i-Martin (1995), *Economic Growth*, New York: McGraw-Hill.

Bourguignon, François and Christian Morrisson (2002), 'Inequality among World Citizens, 1820–1992', *American Economic Review*, 92.4, 727–44.

Bretschger, Lucas and Frank Hettich (2002), 'Globalisation, Capital Mobility and Tax Competition: Theory and Evidence for OECD Countries', *European Journal of Political Economy* 18, 695–716.

Budge, Ian (1996), *New Challenge of Direct Democracy*, Cambridge: Polity, 1996.

Cameron, David R. (1978), 'The Expansion of the Public Economy: A Comparative Analysis', *American Political Science Review* 72.4, 1243–61.

DOI: 10.1057/9781137432674.0010

Clarke, Harold D., David Sanders, Marianne C. Stewart and Paul Whitely (2004), *Political Choice in Britain*, Oxford: Oxford University Press.

——. (2009), *Performance Politics and the British Voter*, Cambridge: Cambridge University Press.

Coase, Ronald (1998), 'The New Institutional Economics', *American Economic Review* 88.2, 72–4.

Dunning, John H. (2000), 'The New Geography of Foreign Direct Investment', in Ngaire Woods (ed.), *The Political Economy of Globalization*, New York: St Martin's Press, pp. 20–53.

*Economist* (2013a), 'Global Trade Imbalances: Fiddling the Data', 27 September.

——. (2013b), 'The Gated Globe: Special Report: World Economy', 12 October.

——. (2013c), 'A Shrinking Slice: Pay and Economic Growth', 2 November.

Garrett, Geoffrey (1998), *Partisan Politics in the Global Economy*, Cambridge: Cambridge University Press.

——. (2000), 'Shrinking States? Globalization and National Automony', in Ngaire Woods (ed.), *The Political Economy of Globalization*, New York: St Martin's Press, pp. 107–46.

Garrett, Geoffrey and Deborah Mitchell (2001), 'Globalization, Government Spending and Taxation in the OECD', *European Journal of Political Research* 39, 145–77.

Genschel, Philipp and Peter Schwarz (2013), 'Tax Competition and Fiscal Democracy', in Armin Schäfer and Wolfgang Streeck (eds.), *Politics in the Age of Austerity*, Cambridge: Polity, 59–83.

Helliwell, John F. (1998), *How Much Do National Borders Matter?* Washington, DC: Brookings.

Hellwig, Timothy and David Samuels (2007), 'Voting in Open Economies: The Electoral Consequences of Globalization', *Comparative Political Studies* 40.3, 283–306.

Hirst, Paul and Grahame Thompson (2000), 'Globalization in One Country? The Peculiarities of the British', *Economy and Society* 29.3, 335–56.

Hutton, Will (1995), *The State We're In*, London: Vintage.

Inman, Phillip (2014), 'Britain's Richest 1% Own as Much as Poorest 55% of Population', *Guardian* 15 May. http://www.theguardian.com/

DOI: 10.1057/9781137432674.0010

uk-news/2014/may/15/britains-richest-1-percent-own-same-as-bottom-55-population.

King, Anthony and Ivor Crewe (2013), *The Blunders of Our Governments*, London: Oneworld.

Le Duc, Lawrence (2003), *The Politics of Direct Democracy: Referendums in Global Perspective*, Peterborough Ont: Broadview.

Lucas, Robert E. (1988), 'On the Mechanics of Economic Development', *Journal of Monetary Economics* 22, 3–42.

Martell, Luke (2008), 'Britain and Globalization', *Globalizations* 5.3, 449–66.

May, J.D. (1978), 'Defining Democracy: A Bid for Coherence & Consensus', *Political Studies* 26.1, 24–38.

Mosley, Layna and Saika Uno (2007), 'Racing to the Bottom or Climbing to the Top? Economic Globalization and Collective Labor Rights', *Comparative Political Studies* 40.8, 923–48.

Myles, Gareth D. (2000), 'Taxation and Economic Growth', *Fiscal Studies* 21.1, 141–68.

North, Douglass (1990), *Institutions, Institutional Change and Economic Performance*, Cambridge: Cambridge University Press.

Ostrom, Elinor (2005), 'Doing Institutional Analysis: Digging Deeper Than Markets and Hierarchies', in Claude Ménard and Mary M. Shirley, *Handbook of New Institutional Economics*, Berlin: Springer, pp. 819–48.

Oxfam (2014a) 'Working for the Few: Political Capture and Economic Inequality', http://www.oxfam.org/en/policy/working-for-the-few-economic-inequality.

——. (2014b), 'A Tale of Two Britains'. http://policy-practice.oxfam.org.uk/publications/a-tale-of-two-britains-inequality-in-the-uk-314152.

Pardos-Prado, Sergi and Iñaki Sagarzazu (2013), 'The Political Conditioning of Subjective Economic Evaluations: The Role of Party Discourse', unpublished manuscript.

Parsley, David C. and Shang-Jin Wei (2001), 'Explaining the Border Effect: The Role of Exchange Rate Variability, Shipping Costs, and Geography', *Journal of International Economics* 55, 87–105.

Piketty, Thomas (2014), *Capital in the Twenty-First Century*, Arthur Goldhammer (tr)., Cambridge, MA and London: Harvard University Press.

Rodrik, Dani (1998), 'Why Do More Open Economies Have Bigger Governments?', *Journal of Political Economy* 106.5, 997–1031.

DOI: 10.1057/9781137432674.0010

Romer, Paul M. (1990), 'Endogenous Technological Change', *Journal of Political Economy* 98, 79–102.

Sandholtz, Wayne and Mark Gray. 2003. 'International Integration and National Corruption', *International Organization* 57.4, 761–800.

Saward, Michael (1998), *The Terms of Democracy*, Cambridge: Polity.

Scharpf, Fritz W. (2013), 'The Disabling of Democratic Accountability', in Armin Schäfer and Wolfgang Streeck (eds), *Politics in the Age of Austerity*, Cambridge: Polity, pp. 108–42.

Sikka, Prem (2010), 'Smoke and Mirrors: Corporate Social Responsibility and Tax Avoidance', *Accounting Forum* 34, 153–68.

——. (2011), 'Accounting for Human Rights: The Challenge of Globalization and Foreign Investment Agreements', *Critical Perspectives on Accounting* 22, 811–27.

Soroka, S.N. and C. Wlezien (2010), *Degrees of Democracy: Politics, Public Opinion, and Policy*, London and New York: Cambridge University Press.

Sperling, Valerie (2009), *Altered States: The Globalization of Accountability*, Cambridge: Cambridge University Press.

Tussie, Diana and Ngaire Woods (2000), 'Trade, Regionalism and the Threat to Multilateralism', in Ngaire Woods (ed.), *The Political Economy of Globalization*, New York: St Martin's Press, pp. 54–76.

Vowles, Jack (2015), 'Government Debt, Globalization, Mass Perceptions of Government Agency, and Political Efficacy: A Cross-National Comparison', in Jack Vowles and Giorgios Xezonakis (eds), *Downgraded Democracy? Globalization and Mass Politics*, Oxford: Oxford University Press, forthcoming.

Whiteley, Paul, Harold Clarke, David Sanders and Marianne Steward, *Affluence, Austerity and Electoral Change in Britain*, Cambridge: Cambridge University Press, 2013.

Woods, Ngaire (2000), 'The Political Economy of Globalization', in Ngaire Woods (ed.), *The Political Economy of Globalization*, New York: St Martin's Press, pp. 1–20.

DOI: 10.1057/9781137432674.0010

# Index

DOI: 10.1057/9781137432674.0011

DOI: 10.1057/9781137432674.0011

DOI: 10.1057/9781137432674.0011

DOI: 10.1057/9781137432674.0011

DOI: 10.1057/9781137432674.0011

DOI: 10.1057/9781137432674.0011

Lightning Source UK Ltd.
Milton Keynes UK
UKOW04n2011261114

242214UK00004B/19/P